Classic
Chain Mail
Jewelry

SUE RIPSCH

KALMBACH BOOKS

Kalmbach Books

21027 Crossroads Circle

Waukesha, Wisconsin 53186

www.Kalmbach.com/Books

Published in 2010

17 16 15 14 13   4 5 6 7 8

Manufactured in the United States of America

ISBN: 978-0-87116-407-0

Publisher's Cataloging-In-Publication Data

Ripsch, Sue.
  Classic chain mail jewelry / Sue Ripsch.

  p. : ill. ; cm.

ISBN: 978-0-87116-407-0

1. Jewelry making–Handbooks, manuals, etc. 2. Chains (Jewelry)–Handbooks, manuals, etc. 3. Chains (Jewelry)–Patterns. 4. Metal-work–Handbooks, manuals, etc. I. Title.

TT212 .R57 2010
745.594/2

Contents

INTRODUCTION 4

BASICS 5

BYZANTINE

Classic Byzantine Bracelet 11

Byzantine with a Twist Bracelet................................ 14

Graduated Byzantine Necklace 16

Romanov with Crystals Bracelet and Earrings.......... 19

Romanov Variations Bracelet.................................... 21

CELTIC

Celtic Line Bracelet and Earrings............................. 24

Celtic Knot Bracelet and Earrings 27

Celtic Variations Bracelet... 29

PERSIAN

Classic Full Persian Bracelet and Necklace.............. 32

Graduated Full Persian with Crystals Necklace 35

Monty Python Bracelet 39

EUROPEAN 4-IN-1

Standard Bracelet 42

Narrow Bracelet 44

Checkerboard Bracelet 46

ESSENTIAL

Box Chain Set.. 51

Double Spiral Rope Set 54

Twisted Ring Link Chain 57

Rosary 60

Sputnik Crystal Earrings 63

3-in-3 with a Twist Chain...................................... 65

Infinity Link Bracelet... 67

Roosa with Gold Balls Bracelet and Earrings 70

Turkish Round Mail with a Twist Bracelet.................. 73

SPECIALTY

Status Link Bracelet.. 78

Dreaming in Mail Set... 81

Crazy Eight Set.. 87

Sassy Swirl of Rings Set 91

FROM THE AUTHOR 95

Introduction

The technique for constructing chain mail jewelry revolves around jump rings. One can go back in history to the middle of the 1st millennium BC to discover when the art of making chain mail began. Initially, craftsmen connected small metal rings by hand to create a mesh that was used as armor material to form a shirt or some other type of apparel that would protect a soldier in battle. The mesh would prevent the tips of swords or knives from piercing the soldier's body. The process of making chain mail armor evolved over time into a method of making stunningly beautiful jewelry.

Nowadays, jewelry artists can connect rings of various metals into designated weaves and designs as well as incorporate crystals, beads, and other forms of "bling" to completely change the look of a classic design. Visual interest is added to pieces of chain mail jewelry by mixing metal types, colors, and textures, as well as by varying the sizes of the wire and the rings. The possibilities are endless!

In this book, I will explain the types of materials and tools used to make chain mail jewelry. I will also explain the basic techniques that are important to know in constructing the jewelry. Written and illustrated instructions will guide you step-by-step through some of the most classic and versatile chain mail jewelry weaves known today. These instructions will list the materials in the amounts and sizes that are needed for the specific project. There will also be a listing of the appropriate tools needed for the project. Most importantly, the actual instructions have easy-to-understand step-by-step directions with photos

demonstrating the different steps. I am a visual person, so I need pictures as well as written words to be able to learn and make a weave for the first time.

Many of these weaves are not original to me, as they have been around for many years, but the instructions are my own. I encourage you to take these weaves and create new and beautiful design variations. There is no limit to the number of variations one can develop from basic chain mail weaves.

Basics

JUMP RINGS

All of the projects in this book begin with a simple pile of jump rings. A jump ring is a circle of wire with one open end. Jump rings are sold by the troy ounce or by the number of individual rings needed for the project. Most suppliers of jump rings identify how many rings of each size are available in a troy ounce, and some suppliers will cut rings to order. Therefore, you will usually buy either a kit that contains the number of rings needed for the project, or a weight in troy ounces of the rings that you will use. Each set of instructions will list what sizes of jump rings will be needed, and how many rings of each size are needed per inch for the piece of jewelry (necklace, bracelet, or earrings).

METALS

There are many different metals one can use to make chain mail. Base metals, which include copper, aluminum, brass, and several others, are great for making jewelry on a budget, but these metals seem to deteriorate fairly rapidly with wear. When I take the time to make a piece of jewelry, I want it to last. Precious metals, such as karat gold and platinum, are wonderful and long lasting, but expensive (gold is a little soft, too). I prefer to use sterling silver, gold-filled, Argentium sterling, and niobium metal rings in my work. These rings maintain their beauty, are durable (although niobium rings should be treated gently with your pliers), and come at a fairly reasonable cost. You can combine these precious metals in a single piece of jewelry for added interest and beauty.

Sterling silver jump rings are usually sold at a reasonable price and are easy to use. Gold-filled jump rings come in the common gold colors of yellow, white, and rose. Gold-filled means that the wire from which the jump rings are made is a hollow tube of gold that is then filled with a metal alloy. All you see and feel with jewelry made of gold-filled jump rings is gold. Pieces of jewelry made from gold-filled rings are very durable, and the rings are easy to work with. The gold-filled jump rings can be made of 10/20kt or 14/20kt. The 10/20kt means that the outer 5 percent of the wire from which the jump ring is made is 10-karat gold. 14/20kt means that the outer 5 percent of the jump ring is made of 14-karat gold. I like to use the 14/20kt wire best, as the jump rings look, feel, and wear like they are solid 14k gold.

Argentium Sterling Silver is an alloy of sterling silver that substitutes the metal germanium for some of the copper content. It does not tarnish as quickly as traditional sterling silver does.

Niobium, titanium, and aluminum are classified as "reactive metals." They're colored through an electrical process, anodizing. These metals are appealing to people who are allergic to other metals and alloys.

JUMP RING GAUGES AND INNER DIAMETERS

Using the correct jump rings is crucial for making any chain mail project, and that means choosing the correct size and gauge. Jump rings have a gauge as well as an inner diameter. The gauge of the ring is the thickness of the wire that is used to make the ring. This thickness generally runs from 12 gauge (very thick) to 24 gauge (very thin), and many points in between. The even numbers (12, 14, 16, 18, 20, 22, and 24) are the most common sizes, although there are some odd-numbered gauges in this range as well. The most common gauges used in chain mail are 16, 18, and 20.

The inner diameter (ID) of the jump ring can range from very small (2.0 mm ID) to very large (13 mm ID or larger) in increments of .25 mm. Therefore, there are IDs of 2.0 mm, 2.25 mm, 2.50 mm, 2.75 mm, and greater. You can even find or have rings cut into other odd sizes.

SPECIALTY JUMP RINGS

Specialty rings can add interest and variety to your pieces. Some examples of specialty rings are twisted rings, which are jump rings made with twisted wire. You can even use two-tone twisted rings, which are jump rings made by twisting a sterling silver wire with a gold-filled wire. Jump rings can also be made out of square wire or half-round wire as well, although half-round rings are thinner, therefore weaker, than their round-wire ring counterparts. Keep in mind that a specialty jump ring may need to be a different size than a round-wire ring in a specific weave.

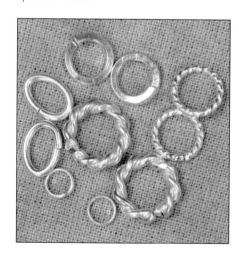

Basics

TOOLS

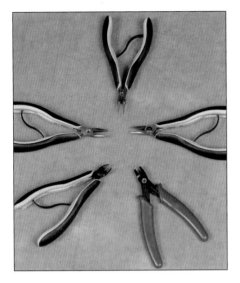

You only need a few tools to begin making chain mail jewelry. You will do most of your work with a pair of chainnose pliers and a pair of flatnose pliers. Some weaves may require other tools, but you can make a lot of chain mail with only those two pliers. For making loops and cutting wire, you'll need a pair of roundnose pliers and wire cutters.

Note: If you already have a favorite tool, then by all means, use it! There is more than one right way to make jewelry, so do what works for you. Some people use a pair of bentnose pliers in place of flatnose pliers. When working with very small rings, it may be easier to use two pairs of chainnose pliers instead of flatnose pliers. Follow the instructions using the tools that are most comfortable.

Be sure that the pliers fit your hands well. If you find that your hands or the palms of your hands hurt or cramp, it may well be that you are using an ill-fitting pair of pliers. The pliers may be too small, too stiff, or have various other problems. (Be sure to use pliers that spring back to the

"open" position.) Having the right tools is important. There are ergonomic pliers on the market that can be quite comfortable to use. These pliers can be a little more expensive, but if you are going to make chain mail jewelry regularly, they may be worth the price.

With many weaves, you may want to use a plastic wire tie or a short piece (4–6 in./10–15 cm) of craft wire to start. Place the first closed ring or rings of the weave on the wire, positioned in the middle of the wire, and then twist the ends of the wire closed. This gives you something to hang onto while starting the chain. Remove the wire at any time.

USING AND STORING JUMP RINGS

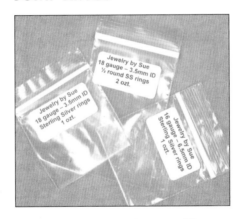

Since jump rings come in many different gauges and inner diameters, it is easy to mix rings of similar sizes accidentally. When you are working on a piece of jewelry, keep the rings in piles that are designated by size, being careful not to mix them.

Store your rings by size and label the gauge, inner diameter, and material. When working with sterling silver, keep the jump rings in an airtight container, such as a zipped plastic bag or a closed plastic container. You can use jump rings

for different projects. if the projects require the same size of ring, so save any unused rings and keep them well labeled for future reference.

CLASPS AND OTHER FINDINGS

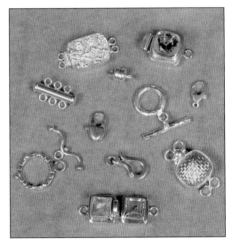

You'll need a few jewelry findings to complete a chain mail piece. You will need a clasp for bracelets and necklaces, and earring findings for earrings. Common clasps are toggle, lobster claw, magnetic, and sliding box clasps. The clasp can be plain or adorned with stones, crystals, or other types of decoration. A clasp often sets off the piece of jewelry, so be sure that it fits with the design. A clasp should also match the weight of the chain so it doesn't rotate to the top of the wrist.

Also, you can find different types of earring findings, such as clip, pierced, lever-back, shepherd's hook, and others. Choose the type of earring finding that is the most comfortable for you to wear. Earring findings can be found in sterling silver, Argentium sterling, gold-filled, and even niobium, as well as base metal findings. Again, choose a finding that is comfortable, easy to manipulate, and works into the design of the piece.

SETTING UP A WORK AREA

You will need good lighting when making chain mail jewelry. A lamp that delivers a daylight type of light is best. This is especially important when working with small rings.

The work surface you use is important also. A work mat of a soft material, such as Vellux, is a good choice. These types of mats can be purchased at most bead stores for about a dollar or two, or you can make them yourself out of an old blanket. This material works well because you can lay the rings on the mat and easily pick them up since the surface is soft and has a give to it.

Be sure that you are able see the rings clearly. Use magnifiers or reading glasses, if necessary, so you can see that the rings are fully closed as you build your piece of jewelry. Safety glasses are a good idea, too.

VARIATIONS

The instructions I share are just the tip of the iceberg when it comes to chain mail design. You can take any of the following weaves and change them to make something new and exciting.

For example, add a watch face in the center of your favorite chain to make a watch. A student and friend of mine, Nancy Maier, wears a medical alert bracelet every day. She builds a length of chain and attaches an appropriately sized lobster claw clasp on each end of the chain. She can then easily attach each clasp to an end of the bracelet and she has a beautiful, yet functional, piece of jewelry.

You can also use your beading skills and add crystals to bracelets and necklaces. Using plain loops, add crystals throughout a necklace or a bracelet, or hang some "bling" from a jump ring on the jewelry piece. Chain necklaces are great for hanging beaded pendants.

Finally, any weave can be a solid color or can be made two-tone. You can add interest by using colored niobium rings or the more unusual rose gold-filled rings.

INSTRUCTION TIPS

Each set of instructions states a total number of rings needed for the project. This number of rings makes a bracelet chain 7 in. (18 cm) long unless stated otherwise, not including the length of the clasp. I will also give you the number of rings needed per inch (centimeter) so you can figure how many rings you need to add or subtract to adjust the length. When a fraction of a ring is needed for the length, I will round the amount of rings up. For necklaces, the length is stated in the Materials List. Again, this is the length of the chain and does not take into account the length of your clasp. I recommend that you have at least a dozen rings of each size over and above the total count of rings listed in case of breakage or loss. For some reason, jump rings sometimes seem to "jump" onto the floor and are then gone forever, so it is nice to have extra rings available just in case. For earrings, due to the small size of the project, a couple of extra rings in each size should be sufficient.

OPENING A JUMP RING

Properly opening and closing jump rings is essential for chain mail. Performing this technique correctly adds to the beauty and durability of your jewelry.

Place a pair of chainnose pliers in your right hand and a pair of flatnose pliers in your left hand. (Reverse these directions if you are left-handed.) Pick up a jump ring with the chainnose pliers, placing the opening of the ring at the twelve o'clock position (or at the top) and the chainnose pliers at the one o'clock or two o'clock position. Then grasp the ring with the flatnose pliers at the ten or eleven o'clock position (close to the opening and on the left side of the ring). Be sure that your arms hang comfortably at your sides and that the pliers appear to be extensions in a straight line with your hands and arms. You are now ready to open the ring.

With your chainnose pliers, pull the end of the ring about ¼ in. (6 mm) toward you. The width of the ring opening varies based on the weave you are making. Some weaves run jump rings through many other rings, so the opening needs to be wider. Other weaves go through only one other ring, so the opening may be narrower. As you are beginning a weave, you will learn what width is

Abbreviations	
ID	inner diameter of the jump ring
in.	inch
cm	centimeter
mm	millimeter

needed and should adjust the opening of the rings accordingly. Always pull the right side of the ring toward you.

The direction that the ring is opened can make a difference when trying to weave the ring through other rings in many weaves. Additionally, the motion used to open a ring is always back-to-front, never side to side. By opening (and closing) rings in a back-to front motion, you can keep the ring's round shape. If you open the ring by pulling on it from side to side, the ring will warp, and it will be hard to get the ring back into a round shape again. If a ring misshapes for whatever reason, discard the ring and use another.

CLOSING A JUMP RING

Hold the ring in the same position with the pliers as you held it when opening a ring. Then with your pliers, move the ends of the ring back and forth (from front to back) four to six times, with the ends just passing the point at which they would meet, until you reach the smallest space possible between the ends of the rings. Don't overdo the front-to-back motion. As you work with rings, you will get a feel for how to open and close them. The ends of the closed ring should be lined up with each other so that the point where they meet feels smooth to the touch.

The ends of the ring may actually touch and make a "clicking" sound when moving them from front to back during closing. This means that you are getting the ends close together and should not have much, if any, space between them when they are lined up. Moving the ends

of the ring back and forth also heats up the bottom of the ring, which hardens the ring. I do not solder any of my rings and do not have a problem with the jewelry coming apart. Chain mail pieces are very sturdy if made correctly. If a piece comes apart, it is generally because you did not close the ring completely and left a gap for the next ring to slip through. It is important to always close your rings tightly and securely.

Thicker-gauge rings will not need as much front-to-back motion to close them as some thinner-gauge rings. You will learn the feel of the different sizes of rings and become comfortable with opening and closing them as you work on different projects. All it takes is a little practice!

WEAVING RINGS TECHNIQUES AND TERMINOLOGY

If instructions tell you to run a ring through the same path, it means that you have already woven a ring into your chain in the appropriate pattern and you are going to run a second ring through the same rings. You then may be asked to run another ring through the same path. This means to take another open ring of the same size and/or metal and weave it through the same rings the previous ring went through and close it. You end up with a ring that is lying beside the previous ring and has gone through the same rings (path) as the previous ring. You can also think of this as doubling the first ring because you are placing another ring beside it through the same rings.

When the directions instruct you to pick up a ring with your pliers, this means to take the chainnose pliers in your right

hand and pick up an open ring from your work mat. You are picking the ring up at the same spot you held it to open it. This means you are picking up the ring with your pliers near the end of the ring (one or two o'clock position on the ring).

In chain mail, you may see in the directions that you have a 2-2-2 chain or a 1-2-1-1 chain or some other set of numbers. Each number designates the number of rings in a row of the chain. Using the examples given, the chain you are working on should have two rings (row one) connected to two rings (row two) connected to two rings (row three), or one ring (row one) connected to two rings (row two) connected to one ring (row three) connected to one ring (row four).

STARTING A WEAVE

Some chain mail weaves are difficult to start. When you are making a weave for the first time, you don't know how the chain should look as you add each ring. This can be confusing and sometimes frustrating, but don't get discouraged. Look at the pictures in your instructions and continue working on the chain. In most weaves, once you have an inch or so completed, the pattern will begin to repeat and make sense to you. Soon, as you work along the chain, you will wonder why as you began the chain you felt it was difficult.

ATTACHING A CLASP OR FINDING

When attaching a clasp or other finding such as an earring leverback or post, use a ring and run it through the attaching ring on the clasp or finding. You may find that when you use one ring between the chain and the finding, the finding may not lie in the correct orientation. If that happens, add a second ring in order for the finding to lie right. Most instructions call for just one ring in a row when adding your finding. For strength or in order to make the design look complete, you may want to double the ring (run another ring through the same path).

MAKING A PLAIN LOOP

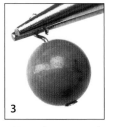

1 Trim the wire or head pin ⅜ in. (1 cm) above the top bead. Make a right-angle bend close to the bead.

2 Grab the wire's tip with roundnose pliers. The tip of the wire should be flush with the pliers. Roll the wire around the pliers' jaw to form a half circle. Release the wire.

3 Reposition the pliers in the loop and continue rolling.

4 The finished loop.

MAKING A WRAPPED LOOP

1 Using chain-nose pliers, make a right-angle bend approximately 1¼ in. (3.2 cm) from the end of the wire.

2 Position the jaws of your roundnose pliers in the bend.

3 Curve the short end of the wire over the top jaw of the roundnose pliers.

4 Reposition the pliers so the lower jaw fits snugly in the loop. Curve the wire downward around the bottom jaw of the pliers. This is the first half of a wrapped loop.

5 To complete the wraps, grasp the top of the loop with chainnose pliers.

6 Wrap the wire around the stem two or three times. Trim the excess wire, and gently press the cut end close to the wraps with chainnose pliers.

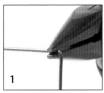

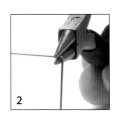

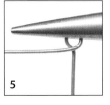

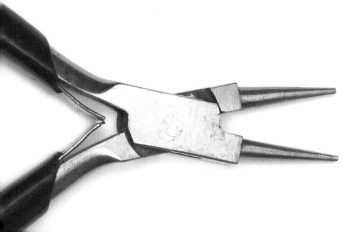

MAKING A FLATTENED CRIMP

1 Hold the crimp bead using the tip of your chainnose pliers. Separate the wires and squeeze the pliers firmly to flatten.

2 Tug the wire to make sure the crimp has a solid grip. If the wire slides, repeat the steps with a new crimp.

MAKING A FOLDED CRIMP

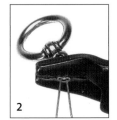

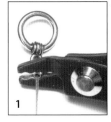

1 Position the crimp bead in the notch closest to the crimping pliers' handle.

2 Separate the wires and firmly squeeze the crimp.

3 Move the crimp into the notch at the pliers' tip and hold the crimp as shown. Squeeze the crimp bead, folding it in half at the indentation.

4 Test that the folded crimp is secure.

Byzantine

Classic Byzantine Bracelet

The Byzantine chain is a true classic in the world of chain mail. It is beautiful, durable, and looks quite complicated, although it is truly a fundamental weave. You are limited only by your imagination!

Materials
- **168** 18-gauge 3.5 mm ID sterling silver rings, 24 rings per in. (10 rings per cm)
- Clasp

Tools
- Chainnose pliers
- Flatnose pliers
- Wire tie or craft wire

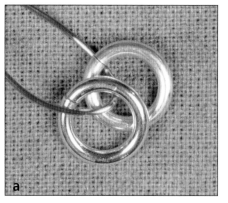

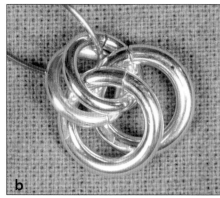

Micro-Byzantine Bracelet

To make a micro-sized bracelet, follow the directions using 252 21-gauge 2.5 mm ID sterling silver or gold-filled rings (36 rings per in./10 rings per cm).

Instructions

1 Open a small pile of rings and close a small pile of rings. Continue to open and close rings as needed while building the chain.

2 Place a wire tie or piece of craft wire through two of the closed rings and twist the ends of the wire closed (**a**).

3 Run an open ring through the two closed rings and close the ring. Run a second open ring through the same path and close the ring. You now have a 2-2 chain (**b**).

4 Run two more open rings through the end set of rings and close them. You now have a 2-2-2 chain (**c**).

5 Grasp the chain and the wire tie in your nondominant hand and flip the two top rings out to the sides of the chain like bunny ears. (These will be called bunny ears throughout the pattern.) Lift your fingertips away and pin the ears with your thumb and first finger to the outside of the chain. Push the flipped rings up a little to position them flat against the sides of the chain (**d**).

Tip: Don't hold the rings too tightly against the chain, as this will make it harder to weave the next two rings.

Aspect Ratio

The aspect ratio (AR) represents the relationship between the wire diameter (thickness, or gauge) and the inner diameter (ID) of a particular size jump ring. If you know the gauge and ID of a ring that works well in a weave, you can use the aspect ratio calculation to change to another size ring that will also work well in the weave. This allows you to make larger and smaller versions of jewelry in the same weave. To calculate aspect ratio, take the ring ID divided by wire diameter (in mm).

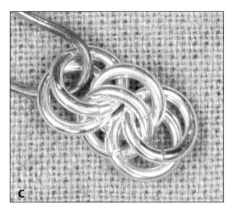
c

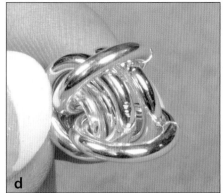
d

e

6 Split the top two rings and insert an open ring *between* the top two rings and *through* both rings (the bunny ears) beneath them. Close the ring.

7 Run another ring through the same path. This locks the bunny ears rings in their flipped down position. This placement of rings is called "locking the fold in place." The last two rings you placed are called the "locking rings" (**e**).

8 Pick up two closed rings with an open ring and run the open ring through the two rings just added to the chain. Close the ring. Run a second ring through the same path and close it. (An alternate method of performing this step is to run an open ring through the end two rings and close the ring. Run a second ring through the same path. Then run a ring through the end two rings and close the ring. Run a second ring through the same path.)

9 With your chain hanging down, you will see that you now have a 2-2-2 chain hanging from the end (**f**).

This includes the two rings that locked the fold in place in steps 6 and 7. This is your signal to go to step 5 to perform the "bunny ears" step again.

10 Continue repeating steps 5–9 until the chain is the desired length. End the chain with the two rings that locked the final fold in place.

11 Attaching the clasp: Run an open ring through the last two rings in the chain and also through your clasp. Close the ring. In the photo you will see that I did this with the loop end of the toggle clasp. You can also use a second ring through the same path if the clasp will accommodate a second ring. Remove the wire tie at the beginning of the chain, run an open ring through the end two rings, and attach the ring to the other end of the clasp. In the photo, you will see that I added two additional rings to the bar end of the toggle clasp. I did this because I needed just a little extra length. (Adding single rings to the weave also makes it easier to fasten the clasp.) You can add length in this manner to almost any of your bracelets if you desire (**g**).

Tip: Add more rings to the chain to make a necklace.

f

g

Byzantine with a Twist Bracelet

This bracelet sparkles and shines wonderfully on your wrist because of the twisted jump rings that are sprinkled along the length of the chain.

Materials

- Sterling silver rings
  - **112** 18-gauge 3.5 mm ID, 16 rings per in. (7 rings per cm)
  - **56** 18-gauge 3.5 mm ID twisted, 8 rings per in. (4 rings per cm)
- Clasp

Tools

- Chainnose pliers
- Flatnose pliers
- Wire tie or craft wire

Instructions

1 Build your bracelet following the "Classic Byzantine Bracelet" instructions on p. 12, substituting the step below for step 4.

2 Instead of running two smooth rings, run two twisted open rings through the end set of rings and close them to make a 2-2-2 chain (**a**).

Use the smooth rings throughout the length of the chain, with the exception of the last set of two rings in each 2-2-2 chain. Always use twisted rings in the third set of two as you did above. This places the twisted rings at regular intervals throughout the chain, adding sparkle and shine. Continue building the chain until it reaches the desired length.

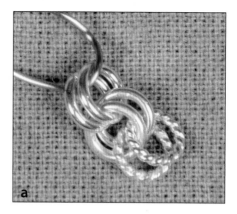

Tip: You can make this a two-tone bracelet by using smooth rings of one color and twisted rings in another color.

Byzantine Squared

Create a bracelet using jump rings made with square wire instead of round wire. Follow the directions for the Classic Byzantine Bracelet, substituting 112 16-gauge 5.25 mm ID sterling silver square wire jump rings (16 rings per in./7 rings per cm) or 168 18-gauge 4.0 mm ID sterling silver square wire jump rings (24 rings per in./10 rings per cm) in the pattern.

Skill Level Advanced Beginner

Graduated Byzantine Necklace

Work from the center to the ends of this graduating necklace for a slinky, showstopping piece. The steps follow the basic Byzantine pattern and are easy to follow—as long as you stay organized! I've also included a necklace with smaller rings for a more petite look.

! Before you begin

Before starting the pattern, read the information below. It will explain how to use the ring sizes. The step-by-step instructions give the large necklace ring sizes with the smaller sizes listed in parentheses.

You are making the necklace from the center working toward the ends, one end at a time. Follow the directions with the ring sizes as listed for the first half of the necklace. Start with the 12-gauge (14-gauge 6.0 mm) rings and weave all of the rings into a single segment following the instructions on p. 18. Then, continue the pattern with increasing sizes of rings, placing half of each size on one end of the 12-gauge segment. The ring sizes and quantities graduate as follows for the first half of your necklace.

Large necklace:

34 12-gauge 7.0 mm rings
(middle segment of the necklace uses all of the 12-gauge rings)

12 14-gauge 6.0 mm rings
(half of total rings)

12 14-gauge 5.5 mm rings
(half of total rings)

12 16-gauge 5.0 mm rings
(half of total rings)

18 16-gauge 4.5 mm rings
(half of total rings, not counting 2 rings for attaching the clasp)

18 18-gauge 4.0 mm rings
(half of total rings)

30 18-gauge 3.5 mm rings
(half of total rings)

50 20-gauge 3.0 mm rings
(half of total rings)

Small necklace:

40 14-gauge 6.0 mm rings
(middle segment of the necklace uses all of the 14-gauge 6.0 mm rings)

18 14-gauge 5.5 mm rings
(half of total rings)

18 16-gauge 5.0 mm rings
(half of total rings)

24 16-gauge 4.5 mm rings
(half of total rings, not counting 2 rings for attaching the clasp)

18 18-gauge 4.0 mm rings
(half of total rings)

30 18-gauge 3.5 mm rings
(half of total rings)

50 20-gauge 3.0 mm rings
(half of total rings)

These rings, with the exception of the 12-gauge (14 gauge 6.0 mm), are for one half of the necklace only. You will build the entire middle segment and half of the necklace on one side, and then switch to the other end of the middle segment and build the other half of the necklace on the other side. Whenever you move from one ring size to another, always begin with the new size of rings as the locking rings that hold the bunny ear fold in place (see step 6 on p. 13).

Materials

Necklace with large inner diameter rings in the center, 18 in. (46 cm)
- Sterling silver rings
  - **34** 12-gauge 7.0 mm ID
  - **24** 14-gauge 6.0 mm ID
  - **24** 14-gauge 5.5 mm ID
  - **24** 16-gauge 5.0 mm ID
  - **38** 16-gauge 4.5 mm ID, 36 rings plus 2 to attach clasp
  - **36** 18-gauge 4.0 mm ID
  - **60** 18-gauge 3.5 mm ID
  - **100** 20-gauge 3.0 mm ID, 24 rings per in. (10 rings per cm)
- Clasp

Necklace with small inner diameter rings in the center: 18 in. (46 cm)
- Sterling silver rings
  - **40** 14-gauge 6.0 mm ID
  - **36** 14-gauge 5.5 mm ID
  - **36** 16-gauge 5.0 mm ID
  - **50** 16-gauge 4.5 mm ID, 48 rings plus 2 to attach clasp
  - **36** 18-gauge 4.0 mm ID
  - **60** 18-gauge 3.5 mm ID
  - **100** 20-gauge 3.0 mm ID, 24 rings per in. (10 rings per cm)
- Clasp

Tools
- Chainnose pliers
- Flatnose pliers
- Wire tie or craft wire

Tip: If you wish to make a longer necklace, add 20-gauge 3.0 mm rings in equal amounts on both ends to reach the desired length. Remember, it takes about 24 20-gauge 3.0 mm rings per in. (10 rings per cm) to make the chain.

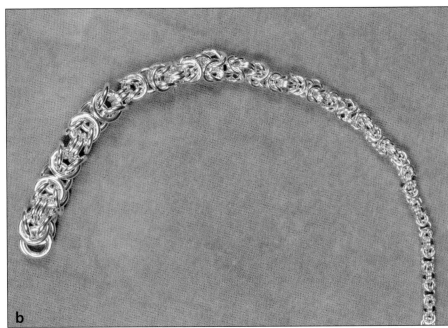

Instructions

Note: Refer to the Classic Byzantine Bracelet for basic chain information.

1 Open 34 12-gauge rings for the middle segment of the chain. Close two 14-gauge 6.0 mm rings. (Open and close rings as needed.) Place a wire through the two closed 14-gauge rings and twist the ends of the wire closed.

2 Run an open 12-gauge ring through the two rings hanging from the wire and close the ring.

3 Run another open 12-gauge ring through the same path and close the ring. You should have a 2-2 chain with two 14-gauge 6.0 mm rings hanging from the wire and two 12-gauge 7.0 mm rings hanging from the 14-gauge rings.

4 Run two more open 12-gauge rings through the end set of rings and close them. You now have a 2-2-2 chain (**a**). Continue using the ring sizes as shown in the chart on p. 17, working from the center out as described earlier.

5 Follow steps 5–9 of the "Classic Byzantine Bracelet," p. 12–13.

6 Repeat steps 5–9 until you have used all of the 12-gauge rings. Then continue the pattern with half of the 14-gauge 6.0 mm rings, then half of the 14-gauge 5.5 mm rings, etc., until half of your chain is complete (**b**).

7 Remove the wire from the end of the middle segment and begin building the chain on this end, using decreasing sizes of rings until you have completed the second half of the chain.

Note: You used two of the 14-gauge 6.0 mm rings at the start of the chain; therefore, you have only 10 more to use when you start the other half of the chain.

8 Using one of the two remaining 16-gauge 4.5 mm rings, open the ring and run it through the two end rings and half of your clasp. Close the ring. Repeat on the other end of the necklace with the other 16-gauge 4.5 mm ring and the clasp. Close the ring (**c**).

Romanov with Crystals Bracelet and Earrings

This variation has a sparkling crystal as a focal piece within a circle of Byzantine chain. The crystals add flash, and it is a treat to wear. Pair with matching earrings to complete the look.

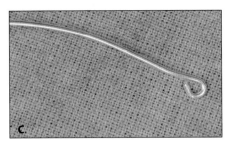

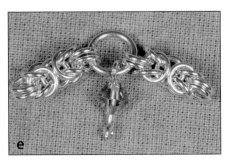

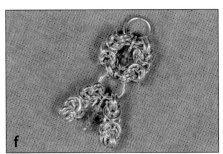

Materials

Bracelet

- Sterling silver rings
  - **252** 18-gauge 3.5 mm ID, 28 rings per flower
  - **12** 16-gauge 6.0 mm ID, 1 ring per flower and 2 rings for connecting the clasp
- **7–10** 6 mm round or bicone crystals
- 12 in. (31 cm) 20-gauge sterling silver wire
- Clasp

Note: Nine flowers equals about 7½–8 in. (19–20 cm)

Earrings

- Sterling silver rings
  - **84** 18-gauge 3.5 mm ID
  - **2** 16-gauge 6.0 mm ID
- **2** 6 mm round or bicone crystals
- 3 in. (7.6 cm) 20-gauge sterling silver wire
- Pair of earring findings

Tools

- Chainnose pliers
- Flatnose pliers (or two pair s of chainnose pliers for the micro version)
- Roundnose pliers
- Wire cutters

Instructions

Bracelet

1 With the 18-gauge rings, follow steps 1–9 from the "Classic Byzantine Bracelet," p. 12–13, ending with a repeat of steps 5–7 where you place a second set of locking rings on the chain. This completes one chain segment, which makes up one half of the flower (**a**).

2 Build a second chain segment that will make up the second half of the flower (**b**).

3 Repeat steps 1–2 until you have 16 chain segments, or the number of flowers needed for the length of the chain (two per flower).

4 With roundnose pliers, make a plain loop (Techniques, p. 9) on one end of a 1½-in. (3.8 cm) length of sterling silver wire, making the loop large enough to fit a 16-gauge ring (**c**).

5 String a crystal on the wire, snugging it against the plain loop. Make a plain loop on the other end (**d**). Make nine crystal components.

6 Open a 16 (18) gauge ring. Place it through an end of one of the chain segments, then a loop of the crystal component, followed by an end of the other chain segment. Close the ring (**e**).

7 Run an open 16 (18) gauge ring through the other end of one of the chain segments, through the other loop of a crystal component, and then through the other end of the second chain segment. Do not close the loop yet. Run an end of another chain segment, a loop on another crystal component, and an end of another chain segment through this same ring. Close the ring (**f**).

You will have one complete flower (including the first closed 16-gauge ring) and half of the next flower on this ring.

8 Continue making flowers until the chain is the desired length for the bracelet. Attach the bracelet to the clasp with an 18 (21) gauge ring. Repeat on the other end of the bracelet.

Earrings

1 Make a three-segment Byzantine chain, running the middle locking rings of the second segment through a closed loop on the end of a wire as in steps 4–5 of "Bracelet." Follow step 6, but before closing the large ring, run it through the earring finding. Repeat to make a second earring.

Romanov Variations Bracelet

Combine the beauty of the Romanov flower components with the texture and airiness of twisted rings for sophisticated style.

Materials

- Sterling silver rings
  - **140** 18-gauge 3.5 mm ID, 28 rings per flower plus 4 rings between every flower
  - **10** 18-gauge 5.0 mm ID, 2 rings per flower
  - **8** twisted 18-gauge 6.0 mm ID
- **5** 6 mm round or bicone crystals
- 12 in. (31 cm) 20-gauge sterling silver wire
- Clasp

Tools

- Chainnose pliers
- Flatnose pliers
- Roundnose pliers
- Wire cutters

Instructions

1 With the 18-gauge 3.5 mm rings, build ten Byzantine chain segments as in the "Romanov with Crystals Bracelet," p. 19. These segments will build five flowers.

2 Make five crystal components following step 5 in the "Romanov with Crystals Bracelet."

3 Open an 18-gauge 5.0 mm ring. Place an end of one of the chain segments on this ring, then a loop of a crystal component on the same ring followed by an end of the other chain segment on the ring. Close the ring. Run another open 18-gauge 5.0 mm ring through the other end of one of the chain segments of the above flower, through the other end of the crystal component, and through the other end of the second chain segment. Close the ring. You will have one complete flower. Run an open 18-gauge 3.5 mm ring through this ring and through one end of the clasp. Close the ring. Run a second 18-gauge 3.5 mm ring through the same path if the clasp will accommodate a second ring (**a**).

4 Run an open 18-gauge 3.5 mm ring through the end ring of the last flower and close the ring. Run a second ring through the same path. Run an open twisted ring through the two end rings and close the ring. Run a second twisted ring through the same path. Run an open 18-gauge 3.5 mm ring through the twisted rings and close the ring. Run a second 18-gauge 3.5 mm ring through the same path (**b**).

5 Make another flower and attach it to the end of the chain as shown (**c**).

6 Continue making flowers and attaching them until the chain has five flowers in it. If you need a longer bracelet, add another flower. If you need a shorter bracelet, remove one of the flowers.

Note: You can also lengthen the piece by adding 3.5 mm rings to the ends of the chain.

Celtic

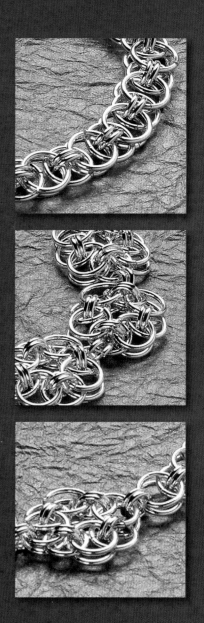

Celtic Line Bracelet and Earrings

The Celtic Line Bracelet has an Irish feel to it. The jump rings form circles within circles that are stylish and appealing. A great everyday piece of jewelry, the bracelet is attractive and comfortable to wear.

Materials

Bracelet
- Sterling silver rings
  - **56** 18-gauge 6.0 mm ID, 8 rings per in.
    (4 rings per cm)
  - **42** 18-gauge 3.5 mm ID, 6 rings per in.
    (3 rings per cm)
- Clasp

Earrings, 1 in. (2.5 cm)
- Sterling silver rings
  - **16** 18-gauge 6.0 mm ID, 8 rings per in.
    (4 rings per cm)
  - **14** 18-gauge 3.5 mm ID, 6 rings per in.
    (3 rings per cm), plus 2 connector rings
- Pair of earring findings

Tools
- Chainnose pliers
- Flatnose pliers
- Wire tie or artistic wire

**Tip: You can use colored rings to add
interest. I like colored niobium, such as blue,
or gold-filled rings for contrast.**

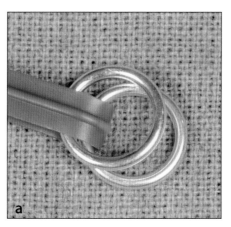

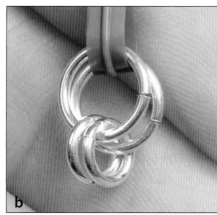

Instructions

Bracelet

1 Close two large rings. Run a wire tie through the rings and twist the ends of the wire closed (**a**). Open a pile of small rings and a pile of large rings. Open rings as needed throughout the pattern.

2 Run an open small ring through the previous two large rings and close the ring. Run another open small ring through the same path. Close the ring (**b**).

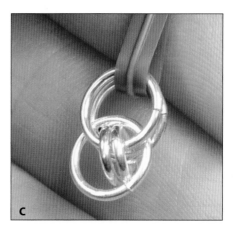

3 Run an open large ring *between* the two large rings and *around* the two small rings. Close the ring (**c**).

Note that this large ring does not go through any rings, but rather *around* and *between* rings. I call this a "floater" ring.

4 Run an open large ring through the two small end rings, being sure that the large ring is lying on top of the floater ring (**d**).

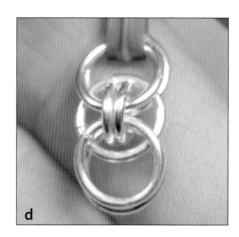

5 Turn the chain over and repeat step 4 on the other side of the floater ring. The floater ring is sandwiched between two sets of two large rings (e).

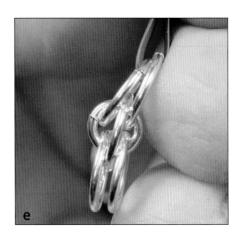

6 Repeat step 2–5 (f) until the chain is the desired length.
Attach your clasp to each end, placing two small rings through the two end large rings and the clasp.

Earrings

1 Weave a 1-in. (2.5 cm) piece of chain using the Celtic Line Bracelet instructions. End the chain with step 5. Attach the chain to an earring hook with two small rings (g).

2 Repeat to make a second earring.

Note: Make the earrings any length you desire by adding or subtracting rings.

Celtic Knot Bracelet and Earrings

The Celtic Knot Bracelet and Earrings offer an interesting variation of the Celtic Line chain. This jewelry gives the illusion of being made of flowers that softly flow along the wrist and hang from the ears.

Materials

Bracelet
- Sterling silver rings
  - **84** 18-gauge 6.0 mm ID, 12 rings per knot
  - **72** 18-gauge 3.5 mm ID, 8 rings per knot plus 2 connector rings per knot and 2 rings for the clasp
- Clasp

Note: The bracelet has about one knot per inch. The photo shows an 8-in. (20 cm) bracelet with eight knots.

Earrings, 1 in. (2.5 cm)
- Sterling silver rings
  - **24** 18-gauge 6.0 mm ID
  - **20** 18-gauge 3.5 mm ID
- Pair of earring findings

Tools

- Chainnose pliers
- Flatnose pliers
- Wire tie or artistic wire

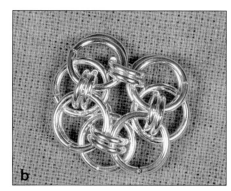

a

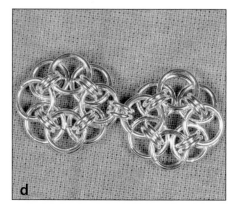

b

c

d

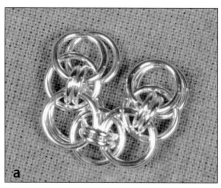

e

Instructions

Make Knots

1 Build a Celtic Line chain as in steps 1–6 of the "Celtic Line Bracelet and Earrings," p. 25–26, until you have used eleven large rings and six small rings.

2 Position the chain flat on your mat in a circular fashion with the ends of the chain close to each other (**a**). Close the circle by running an open small ring through the rings on both ends of the chain. Run a second small ring through the same path (**b**).

3 Place an open large ring into the floater position *around* the last two added small rings as you did in step 3 for "Celtic Line Bracelet and Earrings." Be sure that the floater ring goes *between* two sets of large rings and *around* the last set of small rings. You have now completed a knot (**c**).

Connect the Knots

1 Continue making knots until you have seven, or the number you need for the length of the chain. Attach the knots together by running two open small rings through either two large rings of one knot and two large rings of another knot OR a floater ring of one knot and a floater ring of another knot (**d**).

Note: Be consistent with this connection throughout the chain.

2 Continue attaching knots to the bracelet. When the chain is the desired length, attach the clasp on each end with a small ring (or rings) through a floater ring and through the clasp.

Earrings

Make two Celtic knots. Attach a knot to an earring finding by opening a floater ring in the knot and running it through the earring finding. Close the floater ring (**e**). Repeat for the other earring with the second knot.

Celtic Variations Bracelet

The Celtic Variations Bracelet is a combination of the Celtic Line Bracelet and the Celtic Knot Bracelet. Use the same sizes of rings to build one, two, or three knots. Then begin building a Celtic line chain and place knots between lengths of the chain as you desire. This bracelet has three knots in the center of the chain. Be creative!

Materials

- Sterling silver rings
  - **66** 18-gauge 6.0 mm ID
  - **42** 18-gauge 3.5 mm ID
- Clasp

Tools

- Chainnose pliers
- Flatnose pliers
- Wire tie or artistic wire

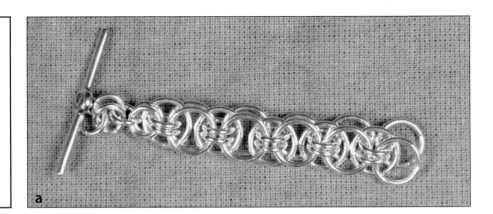

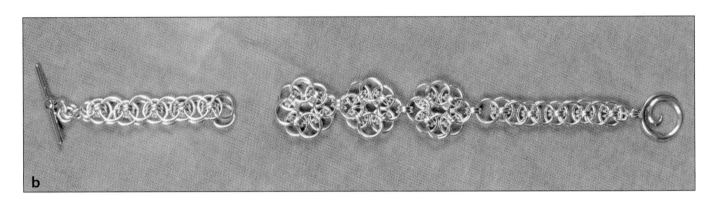

Instructions

1 Follow steps 1–6 of the "Celtic Line Bracelet and Earrings," p. 25–26, until you have 2 in. (5 cm) of chain. Attach one half of the clasp to the end of the chain. This completes the line portion of one end of the bracelet (**a**).

2 Repeat step 1 and create a second separate 2-in. (5 cm) length of chain for the other end of the bracelet. Attach the other end of your clasp.

3 Complete steps 1–3 of the "Celtic Knot Bracelet and Earrings," p. 28, making a total of three knots, and link them together ("Connect the Knots," step 1, p. 28).

4 Attach one of the 2-in. strips of chain to one of the end knots with two small rings. Attach the second 2-in. strip of chain to the other end of the knot with two small rings (**b**).

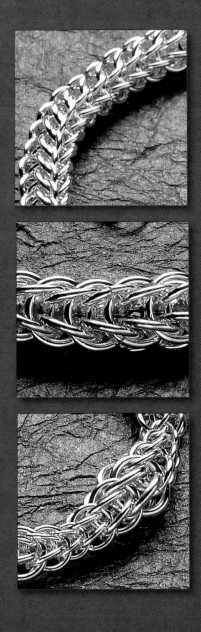

Persian

Persian

Classic Full Persian Bracelet and Necklace

This necklace originates from an old chain mail weave and is the base for the other chains in this chapter. This weave can be constructed from several different gauges of rings, and the smallest gauge of ring builds a chain that looks similar to a snake chain. The jewelry is very smooth to the touch and feels great against the skin.

Materials

Standard bracelet
- **170** 19-gauge 5.0 mm ID sterling silver rings, 24 rings per in. (10 rings per cm)
- Clasp

Micro bracelet
- **308** 24 gauge 2.75 mm ID sterling silver rings, 44 rings per in. (18 rings per cm)
- Clasp

Standard necklace, 18 in. (46 cm)
- **432** 19-gauge 5.0 mm ID sterling silver rings, 24 rings per in. (10 rings per cm)
- Clasp

Micro necklace, 18 in. (46 cm)
- **792** 24-gauge 2.75 mm ID sterling silver rings, 44 rings per in. (18 rings per cm)
- Clasp

Tools
- Chainnose pliers
- Flatnose pliers
- Wire tie or artistic wire

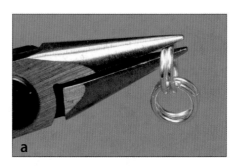

a

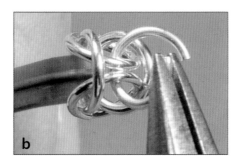

b

c

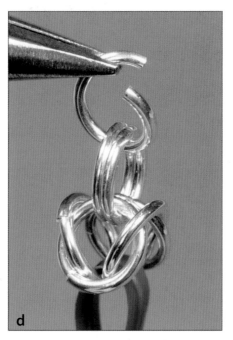

d

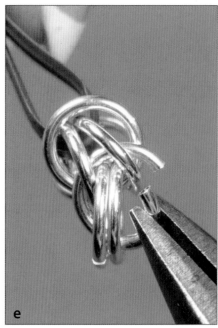

e

Instructions

1 Open about 20 rings and close two rings. Continue opening and closing rings as needed as you work along the length of the bracelet. Run an open ring through the two closed rings and close the ring. Run a second ring through the same path and close the ring. You now have a 2-2 chain (**a**). Run a wire tie through the two closed rings. Twist the end of the wire shut.

2 Flip the top two rings down, split the next pair of rings, and place an open ring between the split rings and through the bottom edge of the two flipped rings (which are now on top) (**b**). Close the ring. Run another ring through the same path and close it (**c**).

3 Place a ring through the top two rings. Do not close the ring yet (**d**).

4 Before closing, twist the ring around and run it through the two rings of the downward-pointing V (see "Which V is Up?" on p. 34), or toward the wire tie (**e**). Close the ring.

Micro Stripes

For a striped piece, use two rings of sterling, two rings of gold, two rings of sterling, two rings of gold, and so on along the bracelet or necklace. For a bracelet in which every other row is two-tone, use four sterling rings, four gold rings, four sterling rings, four gold rings, and so on across the chain.

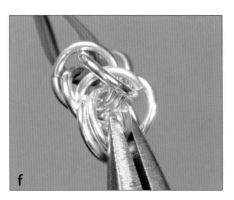

f

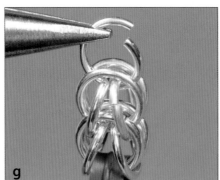

g

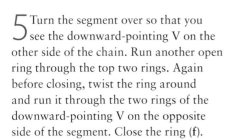

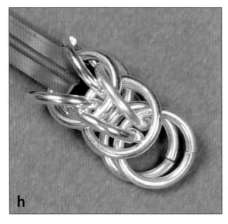

h

5 Turn the segment over so that you see the downward-pointing V on the other side of the chain. Run another open ring through the top two rings. Again before closing, twist the ring around and run it through the two rings of the downward-pointing V on the opposite side of the segment. Close the ring (**f**).

6 Split the top two rings and place an open ring through the two rings in the center of the split rings (**g**). Close the ring. Run another ring through the same path (**h**).

7 Continue repeating steps 3–6 until the bracelet or necklace is the desired length, taking into account the length of the clasp. Add a clasp to each end.

Which V is Up?

In the photo above left, the Vs are pointing downward. In the photo above right, the bracelet has been turned on its side, and now the Vs (gold rings) are pointing upward.

The piece will have two sides of Vs going one direction and two sides of Vs going the other direction.

Skill Level Advanced

Graduated Full Persian with Crystals Necklace

A masterpiece to behold, this stunning necklace shimmers and sparkles from within. Crystals are the secret to the subtle glimpse of color.

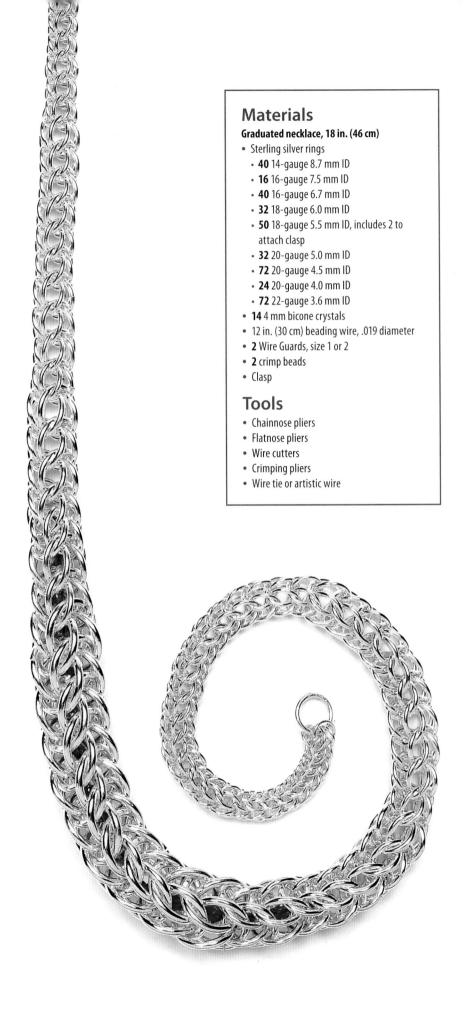

It is important to follow the directions using the ring sizes as stated below. Try to visualize and understand the placement of the ring sizes before you begin.

Begin with the 22-gauge rings and weave all of the rings in the order and amounts listed, following the instructions below.

First half
of the necklace:

36 22-gauge 3.6 mm rings
12 20-gauge 4.0 mm rings
36 20-gauge 4.5 mm rings
16 20-gauge 5.0 mm rings
24 18-gauge 5.5 mm rings
16 18-gauge 6.0 mm rings
20 16-gauge 6.7 mm rings (will connect the beading wire here as in steps 6–7)
8 16-gauge 7.5 mm rings (will have 2 crystals inside these rings)

Middle segment
of the necklace:

40 14-gauge 8.7 mm rings (segment contains 10 crystals)

Second half
of the necklace:

8 16-gauge 7.5 mm rings (will have 2 crystals inside these rings)
20 16-gauge 6.7 mm rings (will end the beading wire here)
16 18-gauge 6.0 mm rings
24 18-gauge 5.5 mm rings
16 20-gauge 5.0 mm rings
36 20-gauge 4.5 mm rings
12 20-gauge 4.0 mm rings
36 22-gauge 3.6 mm rings

Materials
Graduated necklace, 18 in. (46 cm)
- Sterling silver rings
  - **40** 14-gauge 8.7 mm ID
  - **16** 16-gauge 7.5 mm ID
  - **40** 16-gauge 6.7 mm ID
  - **32** 18-gauge 6.0 mm ID
  - **50** 18-gauge 5.5 mm ID, includes 2 to attach clasp
  - **32** 20-gauge 5.0 mm ID
  - **72** 20-gauge 4.5 mm ID
  - **24** 20-gauge 4.0 mm ID
  - **72** 22-gauge 3.6 mm ID
- **14** 4 mm bicone crystals
- 12 in. (30 cm) beading wire, .019 diameter
- **2** Wire Guards, size 1 or 2
- **2** crimp beads
- Clasp

Tools
- Chainnose pliers
- Flatnose pliers
- Wire cutters
- Crimping pliers
- Wire tie or artistic wire

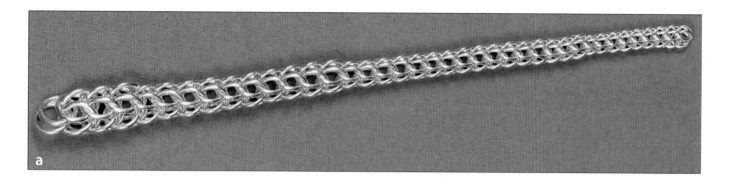

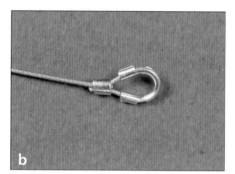

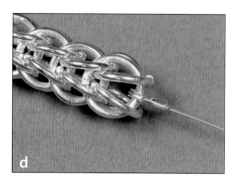

Glamorous Glitter

I love the subtle sparkle of crystals trapped inside a silver cage.

Instructions

1 Open rings as needed throughout the pattern. Start with two closed 22-gauge 3.6 mm rings. Run a wire through them and twist the end of the wire closed. Continuing with the ring sizes in the progression listed on the previous page, run an open ring through the first two rings and close the ring. Run another open ring through the same path and close the ring. You now have a 2-2 chain with a wire through the end.

2 Follow steps 2–6 from "Classic Full Persian Bracelet and Necklace," p. 33–34.

3 Repeat steps 3–6 from "Classic Full Persian Bracelet and Necklace" until you have woven the rings for the first half of the chain. Weave all of the 22-gauge, 20-gauge, and 18-gauge rings, along with 14 of the 16-gauge 6.7 mm rings (a).

You can remove the wire and add the clasp at any time after the chain is long enough for you to hold on to. Use an 18-gauge 5.5 mm ring as in step 6 of "Classic Full Persian Bracelet and Necklace," and attach the clasp to the end of the chain before closing the ring.

4 Cut a 12-in. (30 cm) piece of beading wire and run it through a crimp, a Wire Guard, and back through the crimp. Crimp the crimp bead. Trim the excess beading wire (b).

5 Follow steps 3–6 from the "Classic Full Persian Bracelet and Necklace" instructions with the fifteenth and sixteenth 16-gauge 6.7 mm rings. As you are running the fifteenth ring through the two end rings, run your ring through the Wire Guard so that it is between the two end rings as shown (c). (You are running your ring through one ring, slipping it through the Wire Guard, and then running it through the sixteenth ring.) Note that both rings are still open.

6 Before closing the ring, follow step 4 from "Classic Full Persian Bracelet and Necklace," and run the ring through the downward pointing V. Position the wire so it protrudes from the end rings. Complete step 5 in the bracelet pattern with another ring as shown (d). With the seventeenth and eighteenth rings, repeat steps 3–5 from the "Classic Full Persian Bracelet and Necklace."

7 Place two more 16-gauge 6.7 mm rings (the nineteenth and twentieth rings), following the established pattern. Keep the beading wire in the middle of the rings in the pattern. You have now hidden both the Wire Guard and the crimp within the necklace.

8 Place the first three 16-gauge 7.5 mm rings, following the pattern. Slide a crystal onto the beading wire and inside the three rings as shown (**e**).

9 Place the fourth 16-gauge 7.5 mm ring, following the pattern. The crystal should now be trapped inside the rings (**f**).

10 Continue placing a crystal within each four-ring segment. As the ring sizes increase, you can place all four rings in the established pattern and then slide the crystal inside. When trapping the crystal inside, it is important to always keep the crystal below the ring you are placing. Continue working until you have placed all of the 14-gauge rings (40 total), two sets of four of the 16-gauge 7.5 mm rings, a crystal inside each set of four rings, and the first two 16-gauge 6.7 mm rings. Then run the beading wire through a crimp, a Wire Guard, and back through the crimp. Crimp the crimp bead and trim the excess wire. Be sure not to pull the beading wire too tight as you are finishing the end with the crimp, or the necklace will be too stiff. If this occurs, you will have to disassemble the necklace to the point where the wire was first attached and put a new piece of beading wire in place.

11 Complete the established pattern for the next set of four 16-gauge 6.7 mm rings, being sure that the first two 6.7 mm rings in the set run through the Wire Guard as on the other end of the crystal section of the chain (**g**).

The photo shows the first four 16-gauge 6.7 mm rings in place with the Wire Guard and crimp hidden inside the chain. Build the rest of the necklace in the established pattern, following the ring sizes and numbers as stated at the beginning of the instructions. Attach a clasp to the other end of the chain with another 18-gauge 5.5 mm ring to finish.

Monty Python Bracelet

The Monty Python Bracelet is an original design that is a wonderful complement to your jewelry collection. This bracelet reminds me of the undulations of a snake—it is really remarkable how it seems to flow along the wrist.

Materials

- Sterling silver rings
  - **24** 16-gauge 6.7 mm ID, 4 rings per segment
  - **48** 18-gauge 5.5 mm ID, 8 rings per segment
  - **48** 20-gauge 5.0 mm ID, 8 rings per segment
  - **28** 22-gauge 3.6 mm ID, 4 rings per segment plus 4 rings for the end of the bracelet
- Clasp

Note: Each segment is a little over 1 in. (2.5 cm) long.

Tools

- Chainnose pliers
- Flatnose pliers
- Wire tie or artistic wire

Luxurious Length

Easily make a necklace by adding segments until you reach the desired length.

Instructions

1 Open and lay in individual piles of four rings each: 22-gauge rings, 20-gauge rings, 18-gauge rings, 16-gauge rings, 18-gauge rings, 20-gauge rings, and 22-gauge rings. These 28 rings represent one full segment of the bracelet. Close two of the 22-gauge rings and place them on a wire tie. Run an open 22-gauge ring through the first two rings and close the ring. Repeat with a second ring to make a 2-2 chain as shown in the photo that accompanies step 1 of "Classic Full Persian Bracelet and Necklace," p. 33. This will use all four rings in the first pile of 22-gauge rings. As you build the bracelet, use the sizes of rings in groups of four in the order stated earlier in this step. Continue building a chain, following steps 2–7 from "Classic Full Persian Bracelet and Necklace." Once you have used all of the rings in the piles, the first segment is complete (**a**).

2 Repeat step 1 to build another segment, using the last set of 22-gauge rings from the first segment as the beginning set of rings for the next segment; you will weave a set of four rings onto the first segment in each size going in this order: 20-gauge, 18-gauge, 16-gauge, 18-gauge, 20-gauge, and 22-gauge.

3 Continue building segments as instructed until the chain reaches the desired length (**b**). Remove the wire tie. To attach the clasp, run two 20-gauge rings through the rings at one end of the chain and through one half of the clasp. Repeat on the other end of the bracelet with the other half of the clasp.

European
4-in-1

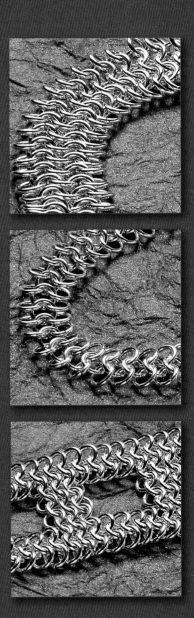

Standard Bracelet

The wide European 4-in-1 weave makes for a sturdy bracelet. This weave originated centuries ago and was used to make protective armor for knights and soldiers. I love wearing it as a bracelet but would not enjoy wearing it as a shirt!

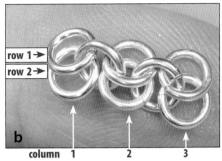

row 1 →
row 2 →

column 1 2 3

b

c

d

e

Materials

- **245** 18-gauge 3.5 mm ID sterling silver rings, 35 rings per in. (14 rings per cm)
- Two-row clasp

Tools

- Chainnose pliers
- Flatnose pliers

Instructions

1 Open 24 rings and close 26 rings. With an open ring, pick up two closed rings and close the ring. You now have a 2-1 chain. Run an open ring through the single closed ring and close the ring. Place another ring through the single ring and close the ring. You now have a 2-1-2 chain. Run an open ring through the two closed rings and close the ring. You now have a 2-1-2-1 chain. Repeat until you have a 2-1-2-1-2 chain (**a**).

This is the base unit from which to build the chain. Note that each two-ring row is a column so there are three columns across the chain.

2 Lay the chain of rings along your forefinger. Be sure that the rings spread in the direction shown (**b**).

3 With an open ring, pick up two closed rings. Run the open ring down through the bottom ring of column 1 and then up through the ring in column 2 of the chain. Close the ring. See the newly closed ring between columns 1 and 2 with the two closed rings hanging from it (**c**).

4 Spread the two new loose rings (**d**). These rings will be the third row for columns 1 and 2 of the chain.

5 With an open ring, pick up a closed ring. Run the open ring down through the third row ring in column 2 and at the same time down through the second-row ring in column 2. Then bring the end of the ring up though the second-row ring in column 3. Close the ring.

6 Position the three rows of rings as shown (**e**).

7 Repeat steps 3–6 for the length of the bracelet. To add a two-row clasp, run an open ring through the end rings of columns 1 and 2, and through one loop of the clasp. Close the ring. Repeat by running a second ring through the end rings of columns 2 and 3, and through the second loop on the clasp. Repeat with the other half of the clasp at the other end of the chain.

Skill Level | Intermediate

Narrow Bracelet

This version of the weave is for the woman who likes a smaller bracelet. Even though it's slimmer, the weave still feels luxuriously slinky.

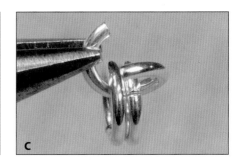

Materials
- **147** 20-gauge 3.0 mm ID sterling silver rings, 21 rings per in. (9 rings per cm)
- 2-row clasp

Tools
- Chainnose pliers
- Flatnose pliers

Instructions

1 Close four rings and open one ring.

2 With the open ring, pick up the four closed rings (**a**). Close the open ring.

3 Lay the rings in the pattern shown (**b**). Note that the middle ring goes through four rings. This is why the weave is called European 4-in-1.

4 Close two rings and open one ring. With the open ring, pick up the two closed rings. Do not close the ring (**c**).

5 Run the open ring down through the bottom ring of column 1 on your chain. Then bring your open ring up through the ring in column 2 on your chain (**d**). (You must go this direction or the chain will collapse.) Close the ring.

6 Arrange the rings as shown (**e**). Spread the two loose rings so that they look like the chain in the photo. Always keep the rings layered in this direction. Repeat steps 4–6 until the chain is the desired length (**f**).

7 Open one of the end rings and run it through one of the loops of one half

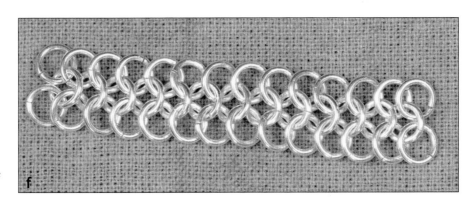

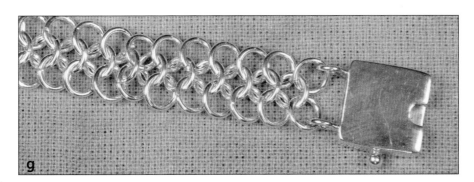

of the clasp. Repeat to run the second end ring through the second loop on the clasp (**g**). Repeat to attach the other half of the clasp to the other end of the bracelet.

Checkerboard Bracelet

The Checkerboard Bracelet is a large statement piece. It has a beautiful two-tone look, although it could be made in just one color. It is very comfortable to wear and elicits many compliments.

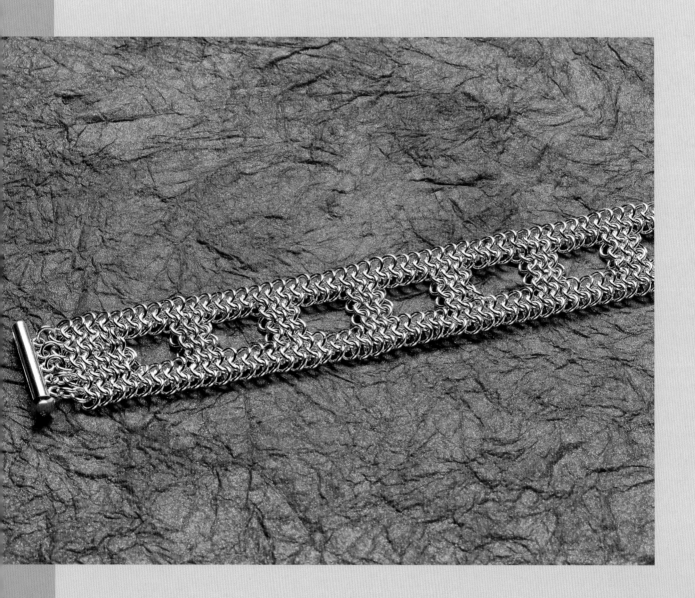

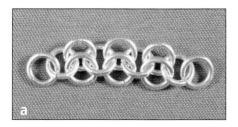

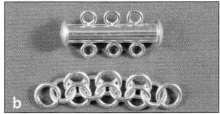

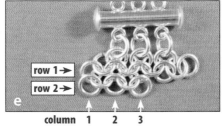

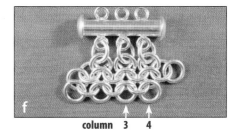

column 1 2 3 4 5

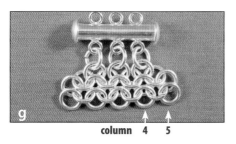

row 1 ➔
row 2 ➔

column 1 2 3

column 3 4

column 4 5

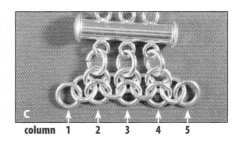

Instructions

1 Open four sterling rings and close eight sterling rings. With an open ring, pick up three closed rings and close the ring. Lay out the rings so that you have a 1-1-2 chain. With another open ring, pick up two closed rings, run the open ring through the two rings on the end of the chain, and close the ring. You now have a 1-1-2-1-2 chain. Continue adding rings in a similar manner until you have a 1-1-2-1-2-1-2-1-1 chain (a).

2 Lay out your chain and three-row clasp as shown (b). With three open rings, attach the clasp (c). It is important to have the rings lying in the right direction.

3 With an open sterling ring, pick up two closed sterling rings. Run the open ring down (from the top of the ring down to the underside) through the bottom ring of column 1 and then up (from the underside of the ring up to the top of the ring) through the ring in column 2. Make sure this ring goes under, not over, the ring connecting columns 1 and 2. Close the ring (d).

See the new closed ring between column 1 (first ring of the chain) and column 2 (third ring of the chain) to the right with the two closed rings attached. Spread the two closed rings so you have one in each column.

4 With an open ring, pick up a closed ring. Run the open ring down through the ring in column 2 of this row and also down through the second ring in the second column in the previous row. Before closing the ring, bring it up through the third ring in column 3 in the previous row. Close the ring. Move the loose ring so that it lies in column 3 (e).

5 Repeat the last step, moving to columns 3 and 4 (f).

6 Move across the row and repeat step 4 with columns 4 and 5 (g). Note the newly added ring (including the closed ring it picked up on the right of it) at the end of the bottom row.

7 Add a ring through the end two rings on the right side of the chain as shown (h).

Materials
- **430** 18-gauge 3.0 mm ID sterling silver rings
- **45** 18-gauge 3.0 mm ID gold-filled rings
- 3-row clasp

Note: If the bracelet is made following these instructions, the chain will be 7 in. (18 cm) long, so consider using a short clasp. I recommend a barrel clasp.

Tools
- Chainnose pliers
- Flatnose pliers

8 Add a ring through the two end rings on the left side of the chain (i).

9 Add a single ring through the end ring on the right side of the row (j).

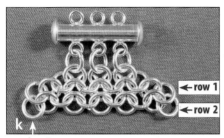

← row 1
← row 2

k

ring 1

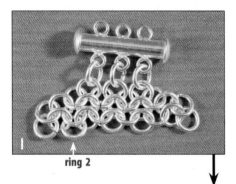

l

ring 2

m

ring 3

n

ring 4

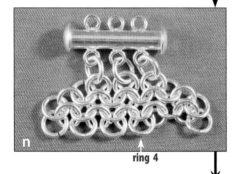

o

ring 5

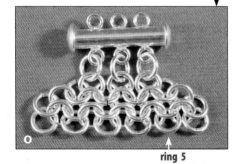

10 Add another ring through the end ring on the left end of the row. This is ring 1 (**k**).

Add rings 2–5 (**l–o**). Each ring is going through two side-by-side rings. You have now completed two rows of the weave, shown by counting two rings in an end column.

11 Repeat step 3 on each side of the chain (**p**). I will call these the left leg and the right leg of the weave. This time, make sure the newly added ring layers over, not under, the corresponding ring in the previous row. Be sure that your weave continues to lie the same way it has from the beginning of the pattern. You are starting the long rows of chain to which the middle or checkerboard pattern of rings will be attached.

12 Repeat step 10 of the pattern down both legs of the weave until you have 6 rows completed on each leg (**q**). (Count the rows by counting on the inside of the rows of three rings you just added. You can continue adding rows to each leg, but I like to attach the two chains now so they have more stability as I work with the rest of the bracelet.

13 Run an open gold-filled ring up through the fourth and fifth inside edge rings for the left leg (**r**).

14 Attach four gold-filled rings in a 1-1-1-1 chain to make a crossbar (**s**).

15 Attach the crossbar to the right leg with another open gold-filled ring, running it down through the fourth and fifth rings on the inside edge of the right leg (**t**). Be sure that the chain of rings is lying in the correct position.

16 Add at least four more rows (total of nine rows) of three rings each to each leg of the weave (**u**).

17 Pick up a closed gold-filled ring with an open gold-filled ring and run the open ring down through the fifth and sixth sterling rings of the left leg and up through the second gold-filled ring in the crossbar. Close the ring (**v**).

18 With another open gold-filled ring, pick up a closed gold-filled ring and run the open ring up through the second gold-filled rings in the first and second rows of gold-filled, and then down through the fourth gold-filled ring in the first row. Close the ring (**w**). This ring is in column 3.

19 Run an open gold-filled ring up through the fourth gold-filled rings in the first and second rows and down through the fifth and sixth silver rings in the right leg of the weave. Close the ring (**x**). This ring is in column 4.

20 Repeat steps 16–18 (but count one row down), and add a third row of gold-filled rings to the crossbar (**y**).

21 Continue adding equal numbers of rows of three sterling rings each down each leg of the weave. I suggest that you add six rows on each leg and then place your next crossbar. Following the established pattern, alternate placing a crossbar of three rows of gold-filled and a crossbar of three rows of sterling rings across the center with the first ring of each crossbar going though the fourth and fifth rows of the legs on each side (**z**).

22 After placing three crossbar sections of gold-filled and three crossbar sections of sterling in an alternating pattern, add four sterling rows to each leg.

23 Start a sterling end section across the middle of the bracelet as you have done previously. This time, add rows all the way across the bracelet for a total of three rows. Then work a fourth end row, using one less ring on each end to form the taper for the end of the bracelet to accommodate a three-row clasp. Attach the clasp to the bracelet with three silver rings (**aa**).

Note: To change the length of the bracelet, add or subtract rows from each end. For a drastic reduction, place only three rows instead of four down the silver side chains between each middle section.

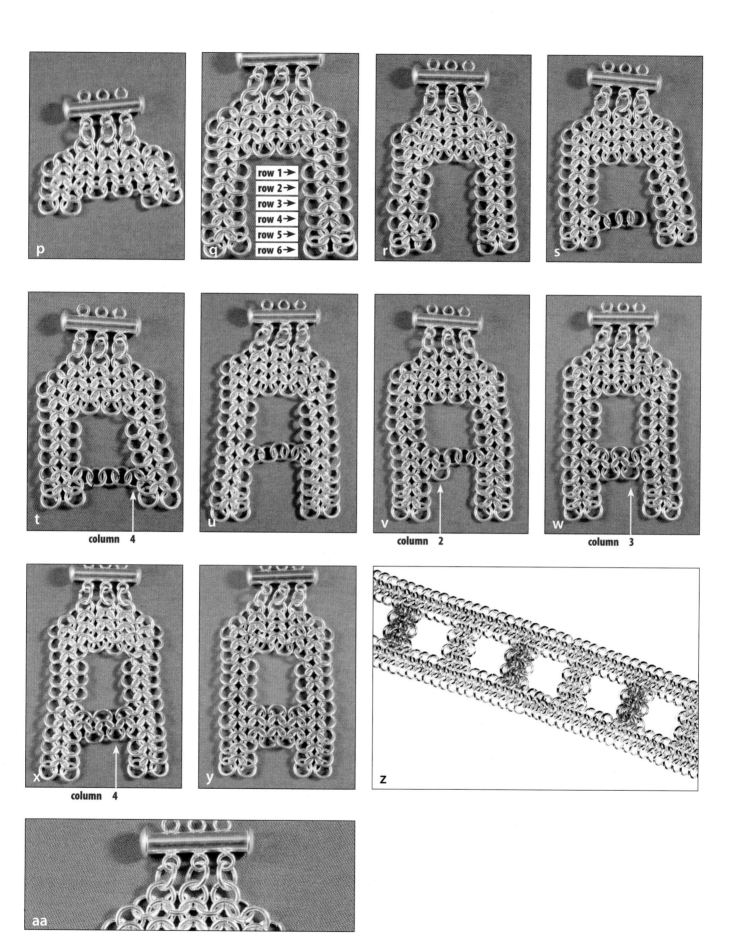

p

q

row 1 →
row 2 →
row 3 →
row 4 →
row 5 →
row 6 →

r

s

t

column 4

u

v

column 2

w

column 3

x

column 4

y

z

aa

Essential

Box Chain Set

Make this sinuous chain into a beautiful bracelet or striking necklace. Hang a bead or charm from the end of the earring chain for added interest.

Materials

Bracelet
- **224** 18-gauge 4.25 mm ID sterling silver jump rings, 32 rings per in. (13 rings per cm)
- Clasp

Necklace, 18 in. (46 cm)
- **576** 18-gauge 4.25 mm ID sterling silver rings, 32 rings per in. (13 rings per cm)
- Clasp

Earrings
- **40** 18-gauge 4.25 mm ID sterling silver rings, 32 rings per in. (13 rings per cm)
- **2** 6 mm beads, charms, or pearls
- **2** 1½-in. (3.8 cm) 20–22-gauge sterling silver head pins
- Pair of earring findings

Tools
- Chainnose pliers
- Flatnose pliers
- Wire tie or artistic wire

Instructions

Bracelet and Necklace

1 Open twelve rings and close two rings. Continue to open and close rings as needed throughout the pattern.

2 With an open ring, pick up two closed rings. Close the ring.

3 Run another open ring through the same path and close the ring. You now have a 2-2 chain. Place a wire tie through the two end rings and twist the wire closed (**a**).

4 Run two more open rings through the end set of rings and close them. You now have a 2-2-2 chain (**b**).

5 Grasp the chain and the wire in your left hand and flip the two top rings out to the sides of the chain like bunny ears. Lift your fingertips away and pin the ears to the outside of the chain with your thumb and first finger. Push the flipped rings up a little to position them flat against the chain (**c**).

Note: Do not hold the rings too tightly against the chain as this will make it hard to weave the next two rings.

6 Split the top two rings and insert an open ring through both rings (the bunny ears) beneath them. Close the ring.

7 Run another ring through the same path (**d**). This locks the bunny ears rings in their flipped-down position. This placement of rings is called "locking the fold in place." The last two rings you placed are the locking rings.

8 Run an open ring through the top two rings and close the ring. Repeat with a second ring. You now have a 2-2 chain including the locking rings in step 7 (**e**). (These steps are the same as in the Byzantine chain, except you will work with a 2-2 chain instead of a 2-2-2 chain.)

f

g

h

9 Repeat steps 5–8 until the chain is the desired length for a bracelet or necklace. Complete the second locking step (see step 7) (**f**).

10 Attach the clasp to each end of the chain with one or two rings (**g**).

Note: For an adjustable-length piece, build a single-link chain on one end of the box chain using the same size rings. Attach a lobster claw clasp to the other end of the chain. You can also attach a small charm to the end ring in the chain, if desired. Clasp the lobster claw anywhere along the length of the single-link chain.

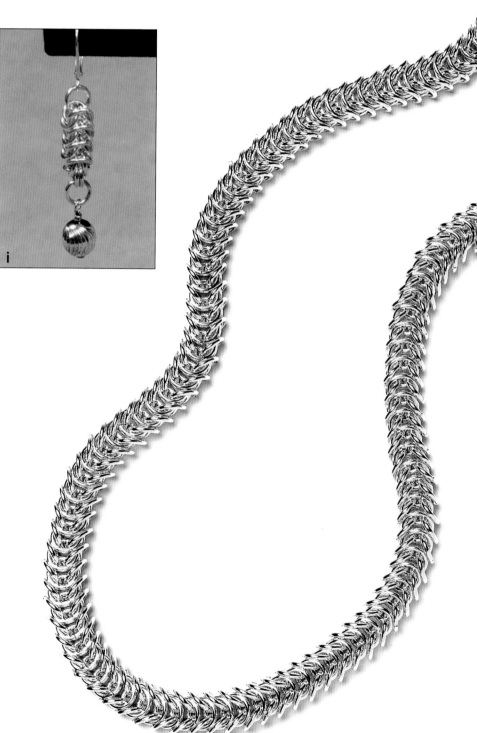

i

Earrings

1 Run an open ring (connector ring) through the earring finding and close the ring (**h**). (This is not part of the pattern.)

2 Build an 18-ring chain off of the connector ring following steps 1–9 of "Bracelet and Necklace."

3 String a bead on a head pin and make a wrapped loop. Be sure the loop is big enough to fit an 18-gauge ring.

4 Run a single open ring through the end two rings of the earring chain and the wrapped loop. Close the ring (**i**).

5 Repeat steps 1–4 to make a second earring.

Double Spiral Rope Set

This versatile and flexible chain makes a great everyday necklace, bracelet, or earrings. Just pick the size of ring (small, medium, or large) that suits you best, and create the chain in that size. Graduated earrings top off the look. Your friends will marvel at what you create!

Materials

Bracelet
- Sterling silver rings
  - Large: **100** 16-gauge 6.0 mm ID, 14 rings per in. (6 rings per cm)
  - Medium: **140** 18-gauge 5.0 mm ID, 20 rings per in. (8 rings per cm)
  - Small: **182** 20-gauge 4.0 mm ID, 26 rings per in. (11 rings per cm)
- Clasp

Necklace, 18 in. (46 cm)
- Sterling silver rings
  - Large: **252** 16-gauge 6.0 mm ID, 14 rings per in. (6 rings per cm)
  - Medium: **360** 18-gauge 5.0 mm ID, 20 rings per in. (8 rings per cm)
  - Small: **468** 20-gauge 4.0 mm ID, 26 rings per in. (11 rings per cm)
- Clasp

Graduated earrings
- Sterling silver rings
  - **8** 16-gauge 6.0 mm ID
  - **12** 18-gauge 5.0 mm ID
  - **16** 20-gauge 4.0 mm ID
- Pair of earring findings

Tools
- Chainnose pliers
- Flatnose pliers
- Wire tie or artistic wire

Instructions

Bracelet and Necklace

1 Close two rings and open about 20 rings in the size you have chosen. Continue to open rings as needed throughout the pattern.

2 Run an open ring through the two closed rings and close the ring. Run a second ring through the same path. You now have a 2-2 chain.

3 Run a wire tie through an end pair of the rings in your chain (**a**). Twist the ends of the wire closed.

4 Insert an open ring into the common space formed when you separate the two pairs of rings (**b**). Close the ring. Run a second open ring through the same path. Close the ring (**c**).

5 Continue to repeat step 4, inserting two rings into the common space formed between the last two pairs of rings (**d**). Add rings until the chain reaches your desired length.

6 Run one ring through the end pair of rings and then through one half of the clasp. Close the ring. Repeat on the other end of the chain with the other half of the clasp (**e**).

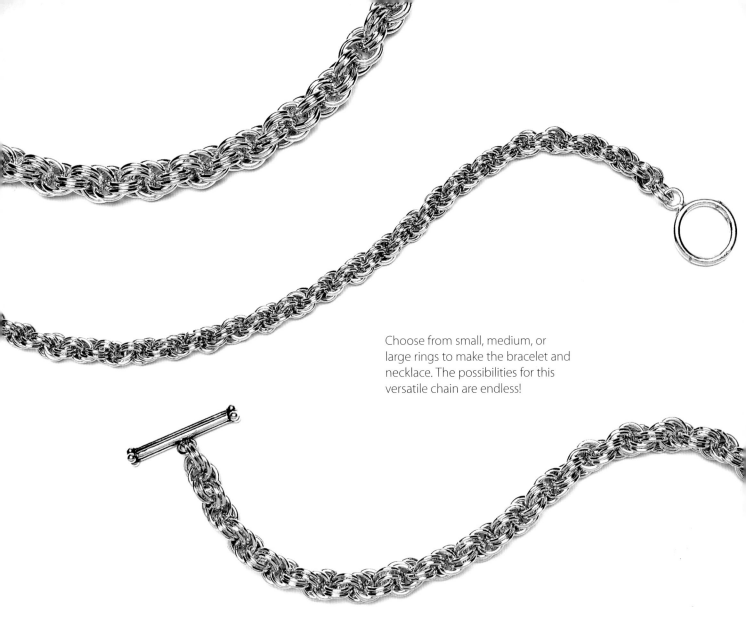

Choose from small, medium, or large rings to make the bracelet and necklace. The possibilities for this versatile chain are endless!

Graduated Earrings

1 Open seven rings in the 20-gauge 4.0 mm size, six rings in the 18-gauge 5.0 mm size and four rings in the 16-gauge 6.0 mm size. Be sure to keep your rings separated by sizes. These rings will make one earring.

2 Place an open 20-gauge ring through the loop in the earring finding and close the ring. This is the connector ring for your earrings (f).

3 Run an open 20-gauge ring through the connector ring and close the ring. Run another 20-gauge ring through the same path and close the ring. Place two

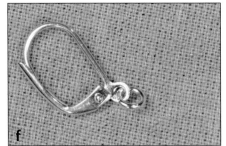

f

g

more 20-gauge rings through the end rings forming a 2-2 chain. Follow step 4 from the Bracelet and Necklace pattern, using all of the rings in each size and continuing with increasing sizes until all of the rings in step 1 have been used (g).

Repeat to make a second earring.

Twisted Ring Link Chain

For an beautiful twist on traditional chain mail, use specialty rings. Suppliers make these rings by twisting sterling silver wire and gold-filled wire together. You can easily add charms along the chain for a truly stunning look.

a

b

c

Materials

Bracelet
- **9** 16-gauge 6.0 mm ID twisted sterling silver and gold-filled rings
- **36** 16-gauge 4.0 mm ID sterling silver rings
- **18** 16-gauge 4.0 mm ID gold-filled rings
- Clasp

Necklace, 18 in. (46 cm)
- **23** 16-gauge 6.0 mm ID twisted sterling silver and gold-filled rings
- **92** 16-gauge 4.0 mm ID sterling silver rings
- **46** 16-gauge 4.0 mm ID gold-filled rings
- Clasp

Earrings
- **2** 16-gauge 6.0 mm ID twisted sterling silver and gold-filled rings
- **8** 16-gauge 4.0 mm ID sterling silver rings
- Gold-filled rings
  - **4** 16-gauge 4.0 mm ID
  - **2** 18-gauge 4.0 mm ID
- Pair of earring findings

Tools
- Chainnose pliers
- Flatnose pliers
- Wire tie or artistic wire

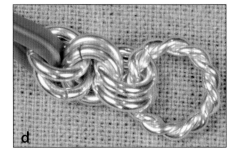

d

e

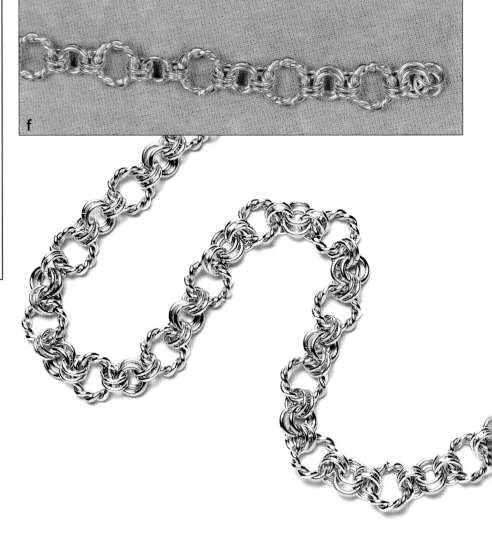

f

Instructions

Bracelet and Necklace

1 Close the twisted rings and two sterling rings, and open all the other rings. (Note that the twisted rings are stiff, so you don't need much back-and-forth movement to close them.)

2 Run a wire tie through the two closed sterling rings. Twist the end of the wire closed (**a**).

3 Run a 16-gauge gold-filled ring through the two sterling rings and close the ring. Run a second gold-filled ring through the same path and close the ring (**b**).

4 With an open 16-gauge sterling ring, pick up a closed twisted ring and run it through the two gold-filled rings at the end of the chain. Close the ring (**c**). Run a second sterling ring through the same path (**d**).

5 Run an open sterling ring through the twisted ring and close it. Run another open sterling ring through the same path and close the ring (**e**).

6 Repeat steps 3–5 until the chain is the desired length for your bracelet or necklace (**f**). Remove the wire tie and attach a clasp to the rings on each end of the piece (**g**).

Earrings

1 Close one twisted ring, and open four 16-gauge 4.0 mm sterling rings, two 16-gauge 4.0 mm gold-filled rings, and one 18-gauge 4.0 mm gold-filled ring. These rings will make one earring.

2 Run a sterling ring through the closed twisted ring and close the ring. Run a second sterling ring through the same path and close the ring (**h**).

3 Run a 16-gauge 4.0 mm gold-filled ring through the two sterling rings and close the ring. Run a second gold-filled ring through the same path and close the ring (**i**).

4 Run a 16-gauge 4.0 mm sterling ring through the two gold-filled rings and close the ring. Run a second sterling ring through the same path and close the ring (**j**).

5 Run an 18-gauge 4.0 mm gold-filled ring through the last two sterling rings and a loop in the earring finding. Close the ring (**k**).

6 Repeat steps 1–5 for the second earring.

g

h

i

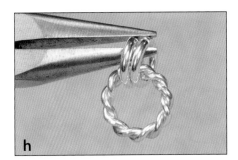

j

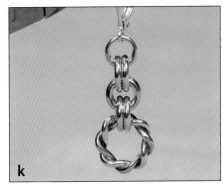

k

Rosary

This Rosary was inspired by my mother, Mary Attig, and I gave her the first one as a gift. It works well as an expression of one's faith, and displays strength and expresses religious commitment. Even if you're not Catholic, the beautiful knots make a gorgeous necklace.

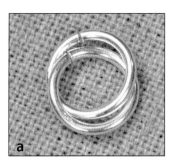 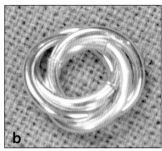 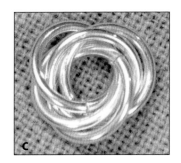 

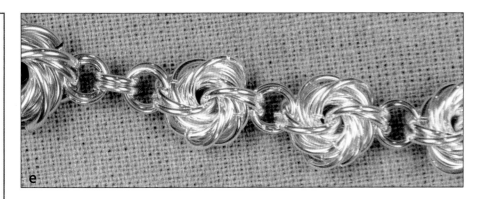

Materials

Standard rosary, 19 in. (48 cm)
- **90** 18-gauge 6.0 mm ID gold-filled rings (large rings)
- **750** 20-gauge 5.0 mm ID sterling silver rings (medium rings)
- **150** 20-gauge 3.0 mm ID gold-filled rings (small rings)
- crucifix and bead station

Petite rosary, 12½ in. (31.8 cm)
- **80** 20-gauge 4.5 mm ID gold-filled (large rings)
- **690** 22-gauge 3.6 mm ID sterling silver rings (medium rings)
- **80** 22-gauge 2.5 mm ID gold-filled rings (small rings)
- crucifix and bead station

Tools
- Chainnose pliers (may want a second pair for the Petite Rosary)
- Flatnose pliers

Note: The lengths of the rosaries given above is the length of the rosary stretched out in a straight line from one end to the bottom of the crucifix on the other end.

Instructions

Note: Throughout the instructions, use 14 rings per knot for the standard and 13 rings per knot for the petite rosary. Make all of the knots at once, or hook them together as you go.

Make a Knot

1 Close one medium ring and open the rest of the medium rings needed to complete a knot.

2 With one of the open rings, pick up the closed ring and close the ring. Nest the rings together (**a**).

3 Run an open ring through the two closed rings and close the ring. Again, nest the rings together (**b**).

4 Continue running each of the remaining open rings through the center of all of the closed rings as described above (**c**). Repeat until you have used up all of the rings for the knot (**d**). Be sure to always nest the rings symmetrically on your mat before running the next ring through the center. This gives you a nicer looking knot, although usually no two knots will look exactly alike.

5 Make has 53 medium knots and six large knots, or the number of knots desired.

Connect the Knots

6 The small rings are the connecting rings between the knots, the crucifix, and the bead station. To connect the medium knots, open some of the small rings. Run a small ring through two rings on a medium knot and then through two rings on another medium knot. Close the ring. Run a second ring through the same path (**e**). Continue connecting medium knots with two small rings between each set until the chain is ten knots long. It is important to connect rings on opposite sides of each knot in order to have the knots lie nicely.

7 The eleventh knot should be a large gold knot. Connect this to the chain with two small rings running through two rings on the last medium knot. Close these rings. Run two more small rings through the last two small rings and close these rings. Run two more small rings

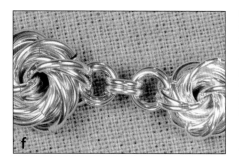

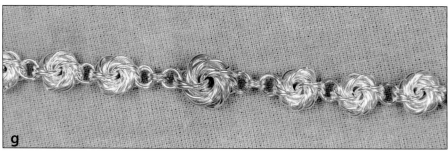

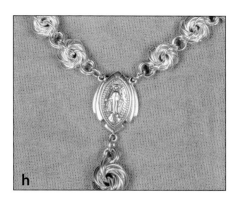

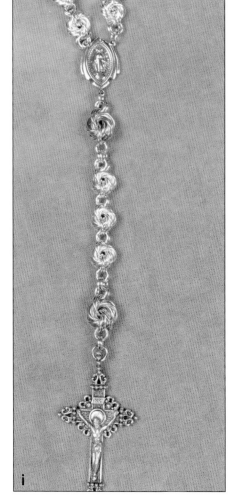

(total of three sets of two small rings in a row) through the last two small rings and also through two rings on a large knot. Close these rings (f).

8 Connect another chain of three pairs of small rings off of the other side of the large knot, being sure to run the last two small rings through two rings on another medium knot (g). Attach nine more medium knots to the chain, following step 1. You now have a chain of ten medium knots, one large knot, and ten medium knots. Continue building the chain in this manner until you have connected five sets of ten medium knots and four single large knots (ten medium knots, one large knot, ten medium knots, one large knot, ten medium knots, one large knot, ten medium knots, one large knot, and ten medium knots).

Bead Station and Crucifix

9 Run two small rings through two rings on the medium knot at one end of the rosary chain. Close the rings. Run two more rings through the two end rings and, before closing, run them through one of the top rings on the bead station. Close the rings. Repeat and connect the other end of the chain to the other top ring on the bead station (h).

10 Make three medium knots and two large knots as before and set them aside.

11 Run a small ring through the bottom loop on the bead station and close the ring. Run a small ring through this ring and two rings on one of the large knots. Close the ring. Run a second small ring through the same path. Again, see **photo h** to attach the first knot to the bottom of the bead station. Attach three medium knots and a large knot to the large knot hanging from the bead station as described above. Run two small rings through two rings on the bottom of the end large knot and close the rings. Run two more small rings through the end two rings and close the rings. You can run either a large ring or two small rings through the end rings and the crucifix. Close the ring(s) (i).

Sputnik Crystal Earrings

These earrings have a very modern "circle" look with the added bling of bicone crystals. The orbital nature of the dangle reminds me of planets and space. They are to be worn, enjoyed, and admired!

Materials
- Sterling silver rings
  - **2** 20-gauge 2.5 mm ID
  - **6** 20-gauge 4.0 mm ID
  - **4** 16-gauge 10.0 mm ID
- **2** 6 mm bicone crystals
- **2** 1½-in. (3.8 cm) 22-gauge sterling silver head pins
- Pair of earring findings

Tools
- Chainnose pliers
- Flatnose pliers
- Wire cutters
- Roundnose pliers

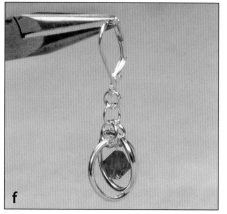

Instructions

1 Open one 20-gauge 2.5 mm ring and run it through the loop in the earring finding. Close the ring (**a**).

2 Open one 20-gauge 4.0 mm ring and run it through the end ring. Close the ring (**b**).

3 Open another 20-gauge 4.0 mm ring, run it through the first 4.0 mm ring, and close the ring. Repeat to add a second 4.0 mm ring. You now have a 1-1-2 chain (**c**).

4 String a crystal on a head pin and make a plain loop (**d**). Be sure the loop is large enough for the 16-gauge 10 mm ring to pass through.

5 Open a 10 mm ring and run it through one of the end 4.0 mm rings, the loop on the crystal, and the second 4.0 mm end ring. Close the ring. The crystal will hang down into the 16-gauge ring with its loop between the two 4.0 mm rings (**e**).

6 Run a second open 10 mm ring between the two 4.0 mm rings going over the first 16-gauge ring. Run the end of the open ring inside of the first 16-gauge ring. Close the ring (**f**).
    Repeat to make a second earring.

3-in-3 with a Twist Chain

Simple but elegant, the twisted rings in this set give off a beautiful radiance and shine that draws the eye to your wrist or ears. The bracelet is substantial but lies nicely along your wrist and is quite comfortable to wear.

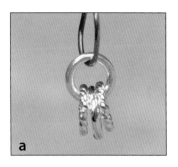

a

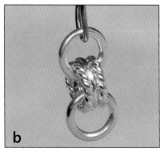

b

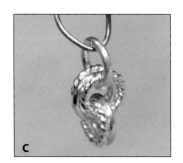

c

d

Materials

Bracelet
- Sterling silver rings
  - **70** 16-gauge 5.0 mm ID, 10 rings per in. (4 rings per cm)
  - **70** 16-gauge 5.0 mm ID twisted, 10 rings per in. (4 rings per cm)
  - **2** 16-gauge 5.0 mm ID
- Clasp

Earrings
- Sterling silver rings
  - **14** 16-gauge 5.0 mm ID
  - **12** 16-gauge 5.0 mm ID twisted
- Pair of earring findings

Tools
- Chainnose pliers
- Flatnose pliers
- Wire tie or artistic wire

e

f

Instructions

Bracelet

1 Close two twisted rings and one smooth ring, and open one smooth ring. Continue opening rings throughout the pattern as needed.

2 With the open ring, pick up a closed twisted ring, a closed smooth ring, and a closed twisted ring. Close the open ring. Run a wire tie through the single closed ring and twist the ends of the wire closed. You have a 1-3 chain (**a**).

3 Run an open smooth ring through the three rings and close the ring. You now have a 1-3-1 chain (**b**).

4 Run an open twisted ring through the three rings alongside the last ring added and close the ring. You now have a 1-3-2 chain (**c**).

5 Run an open smooth ring through the three rings alongside the last ring added so that the twisted ring is between the two smooth rings. Close the ring. You now have a 1-3-3 chain (**d**).

Note: Notice how the first set of three rings is composed of a twisted-smooth-twisted ring combination and the second set of three rings is a smooth-twisted-smooth combination. You will alternate these two combinations throughout the length of the bracelet.

6 Continue adding rings as in steps 3–5, alternating the two-ring combinations. Build the chain to the desired length.

7 On each end of the chain, use a single ring to attach the clasp (**e**).

Note: Change the ring combination, using all smooth rings or all twisted rings, or even making the bracelet two-tone if desired. Remember that the chain uses almost seven sets of three

rings per inch in whatever combination of rings chosen.

Earrings

1 Follow steps 1–5 of the bracelet instructions. You will have a 1-3-3 chain in an alternating combination of twisted-smooth-twisted and smooth-twisted-smooth rings.

2 Repeat steps 3–6 of "Bracelet" until you have a 1-3-3-3-3 chain in the alternating sets of three rings as in the bracelet instructions.

3 Remove the wire tie. Open the ring that was on the wire and run it through the loop in an earring finding. Close the ring (**f**). Repeat steps 1–3 to make a second earring.

Note: Make the earrings longer or shorter by adding or removing additional sets of three rings to the chain.

Infinity Link Bracelet

Light and airy, this bracelet is unique to every jewelry maker, as each infinity knot will look different. Choose a stunning clasp to finish the piece.

Materials

- **105** 18-gauge 4.0 mm ID sterling silver rings, 15 rings per in. (6 rings per cm)
- Clasp

Note: You could easily make this weave into a necklace by adding more rings. An 18-in. (46 cm) necklace would use 270 rings.

Tools

- Chainnose pliers
- Flatnose pliers
- Wire tie or artistic wire

Instructions

1 Open six rings and close two rings. Continue opening rings as needed throughout the pattern. With an open ring, pick up the two closed rings. Close the ring. You now have a 1-2 chain. Run a wire tie through the single ring and twist the ends closed (**a**).

2 Run an open ring through the two end rings and close the ring. Run a second ring through the same path. You now have a 1-2-2 chain (**b**).

3 Position the rings in your hand as shown (**c**). The two rings that are connected to the single ring should lie flat and the two end rings should be pushed up.

4 Run an open ring through the first set of two rings as shown (**d**). Note the location of the pliers tips on the end of the ring.

5 Remove the tips of the pliers from the end of the ring they are holding and grasp the other end of the ring with the pliers (**e**).

6 Swing the free end of the open ring up and through the top two rings

(end rings) in the chain (**f**). Follow the movement between **photo e** and **photo f**.

7 Close the ring (**g**). The newly added ring is shown held by the pliers.

8 Run a second ring through the same path. Close the ring (**h**). This completes one infinity knot (the set of 2-2-2 rings form the knot).

9 Insert a single open ring through the last two rings you added to the knot. Close the open ring. The single connector ring on the end of the first knot segment serves as the connector ring for the beginning of the next knot segment.

10 Run two open rings through the end ring and close the rings (**i**). You now have a 1-2 chain to start your next knot segment as you did in step 1.

11 Run two more open rings through the last two rings and close the rings (**j**). You now have a 1-2-2 chain as you did in step 2.

12 Repeat steps 3–9 to complete the next knot segment. Continue with the pattern and connect knots until you reach your desired length (**k**).

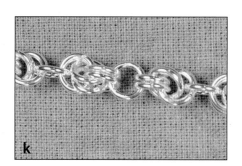

13 End the pattern with a single connector ring. Attach the clasp on each end by opening the end single ring and running it through the loop of the clasp. Close the ring (l). You could also run a second ring through the end single ring and through the clasp.

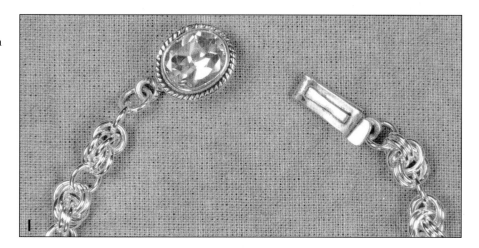

Skill Level Advanced Beginner

Roosa with Gold Balls Bracelet and Earrings

Gold balls add movement and interest to chain mail. This set is easy to make and fun to wear. People will ask where you purchased these pieces of jewelry!

Materials

Bracelet
- **56** 18-gauge 5.5 mm ID sterling silver rings, 8 rings per in. (3 rings per cm)
- **28** 18-gauge 5.5 mm ID gold-filled rings, 4 rings per in. (2 rings per cm)
- **28** 5 mm gold-filled round beads
- Clasp

Earrings
- **18** 18-gauge 5.5 mm ID sterling silver rings
- **12** 18-gauge 5.5 mm ID gold-filled rings
- **2** 18-gauge 3.5 mm ID sterling silver rings
- **10** 5 mm gold-filled round beads
- Pair of ear wires

Tools
- Chainnose pliers
- Flatnose pliers
- Wire tie or artistic wire

Instructions

Bracelet

1 Open some sterling and some gold-filled rings. Close two gold-filled rings and run a wire through them. Twist the ends of the wire closed. Run an open sterling ring through the two gold-filled rings on the wire. Close the ring. Run another ring through the same path. You now have a 2-2 chain (**a**).

2 Continue adding two rings in alternating colors to the end of the chain until you reach the desired length (**b**). This will make a 2-2-2-2-2 chain, with the number of rows of double rings dependent upon the length of the bracelet.

Note: You can also build the chain as you go along rather than building the entire length of the chain first.

3 String a gold-filled bead on an open sterling ring. Do not close the ring. With this ring, go between the first two sterling rings in the chain and also through one of the gold-filled rings that is hanging from the wire (**c, d**). Close the ring.

Note: Photo c shows how the sterling ring goes between the two other sterling rings. The ring is going through one gold-filled ring but also between the two gold-filled rings in the chain. **Photo d** shows the same step from a different angle.

4 Repeat step 3 with another sterling and gold-filled ring, this time working on the other side of the chain (**e**). This means that you are going between the same two sterling rings on the other side of the chain, and that you are also going through the other gold-filled ring that the last sterling with gold-filled ring did not go through.

5 Moving down the chain, continue adding the sterling with gold-filled rings through the bottom edge of each pair of gold-filled rings and between the pairs of sterling rings as in steps 3–4 (**f**).

6 End the chain with a single sterling ring through a pair of gold-filled rings. Run another gold-filled ring through the sterling ring and the clasp. Close the ring. Repeat at the other end of the chain by adding rings of either color (**g**).

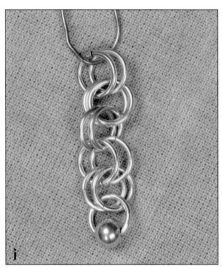

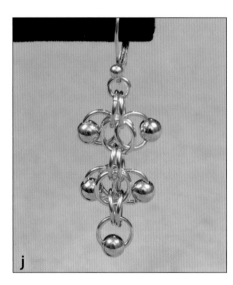

Earrings

1 Open nine 5.5 mm ID sterling and six gold-filled rings. Also open an 18-gauge 3.5 mm ID sterling ring. Set five gold-filled beads beside these rings. This quantity of rings and beads will make one earring.

2 With 5.5 mm sterling and gold-filled rings, build a 2-2-2-2-2 chain as you did for the bracelet, starting with two

gold-filled rings and ending with two gold-filled rings in the chain (**h**). Place a wire tie through the two rings on one end of the chain and twist the wire shut.

3 Run a gold-filled bead onto an open 5.5 mm sterling ring. Run it through the end two gold-filled rings and close the ring (**i**). This is the bottom of the earring.

4 Repeat steps 3–4 of "Bracelet" twice.

5 Remove the wire and run the 3.5 mm sterling ring through these two end rings and through the loop in an earring finding. Close the ring (**j**). Repeat to make a second earring.

Turkish Round Mail with a Twist Bracelet

This sparkling variation of the Turkish Round Mail weave is very comfortable to wear. Twisted rings sprinkled along the length of the bracelet add glimmer and shine.

Materials

- **170** 18-gauge 3.5 mm ID sterling silver smooth rings, 24 rings per in. (10 rings per cm)
- **84** 18-gauge 3.5 mm ID sterling silver twisted rings, 12 rings per in. (5 rings per cm)
- Clasp

Tools

- Chainnose pliers
- Flatnose pliers
- Wire tie or artistic wire

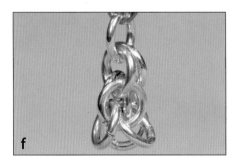

Instructions

1. Open eight smooth rings and close one smooth ring. Pick up the closed ring with an open ring, and then close the open ring. Place another open ring through the original closed ring and close. This forms a 1-2 chain. Place a wire tie through the single ring. Twist the wire tie closed (**a**).

2. Place one open ring through the two closed end rings. Close the ring. This gives you a 1-2-1 chain (**b**).

3. Place an open ring through one ring in the pair of rings in the 1-2-1 chain. Close the ring. You now have a 1-2-2 chain.

4. Place another open ring through the other ring in the pair of rings in the 1-2-1 (which became a 1-2-2 chain in step 3). Close the ring. You now have a 1-2-3 chain (**c**).

5. Pick up an open ring and run it through two adjacent edge rings in the row of three rings. Close the ring (**d**).

   Although it is difficult to see all three rings in the third row in the photo, be sure to place the open ring through the edges of two adjacent rings in that row. Pick up a second open ring, run it through two other adjacent ring edges in the row of three rings, and close it (**e**).

   Pick up a third open ring, run it through the last two adjacent ring edges in the bottom row, and close it (**f**).

Note: You now have a triangle formed by the last row of three rings. The three rings are positioned to hold the triangle together. You may need to move the three rings placed in step 4 around in order to get them in a triangle formation. Once you have the triangle established in this step, it will automatically be positioned for you in the next steps.

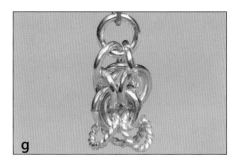

g

h

6 Open three twisted rings. Repeat step 5 on the bottom row of rings in the chain using the twisted open rings (**g**). You now have three rows of three rings each, with the last row composed of three twisted rings.

i

j

7 Open six smooth rings and three twisted rings and lay them out in rows of three—two rows of smooth rings and a final row of twisted rings. Laying your rings in rows as you open them will help you keep your place in the pattern.

8 Flip the twisted rings at the end of the chain back toward the start of the chain. **Photo h** shows them starting to be flipped back, and **photo i** shows them flipped back and held. Note the bottom edges (which are now the top edges) of the twisted rings in the middle of the three smooth rings in the picture.

k

9 Choosing from the three rows of open rings laid out in step 7, pick up one open smooth ring and run it through the new top edges of two twisted rings in the chain (**j**).

Place an open smooth ring through two other twisted rings and close. Repeat a third time, forming a triangle with your smooth rings (**k**). The smooth rings lock the fold in place. See how the chain looks when holding it downward (**l**).

l

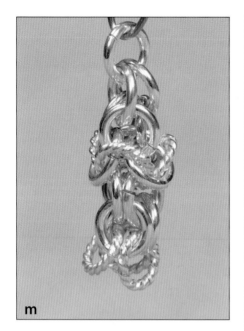

m

n

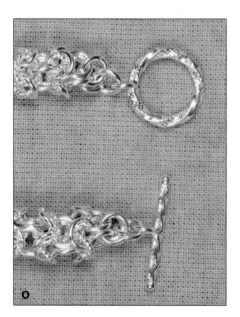

o

10 Repeat steps 5–6 with the other two rows of open smooth rings and then the remaining row of twisted rings (**m**).

11 Again, lay out open rings in groups of three rings in three rows as in step 7. Repeat steps 8–9. (Your pattern is two rows of three smooth rings and one row of three twisted rings. You flip the twisted rings and with the first row of the next set of smooth rings, lock the fold in place.) Repeat this pattern along the length of the chain (**n**).

12 End with a row that locks a flip row into place when you are at your desired length, taking into account the length of the clasp. Then, using two open smooth rings, place one to connect two of the smooth rings together from the last row and close the ring. Place the second ring through the third smooth ring plus one other ring in the last row and close the ring. This forms a row of two rings. Then place one open smooth ring through the two rings in the last row and run it through one half of the clasp. Close the ring (**o**). (You will end with a three-ring row and a double ring row followed by a single ring row, as you did at the beginning of the chain.) Open the single ring on the other end of the bracelet and attach the other half of the clasp.

Make a Classic Turkish Round Mail Bracelet by substituting smooth rings for the twisted rings.

Specialty

Status Link Bracelet

This original design adds movement and grace to your wrist. The addition of the twisted rings adds an extra measure of detail to the jewelry. It is fresh and modern.

Materials

- Sterling silver rings
  - **28** 16-gauge 5.5 mm ID, 4 rings per in. (2 rings per cm)
  - **28** 16-gauge 6.0 mm ID, 4 rings per in. (2 rings per cm)
  - **6** 18-gauge 3.5 mm ID for the clasp
  - **21** 16-gauge 6.0 mm ID twisted, 3 rings per in. (2 rings per cm)
  - **14** 16-gauge 9.6 mm oval, 2 rings per in. (1 ring per cm)
- Clasp

Tools

- Chainnose pliers
- Flatnose pliers
- Wire tie or artistic wire

Note: Oval rings are difficult to close tightly. Don't worry if they don't close all the way, as the rolling rings will cover the oval ring and hide the gap.

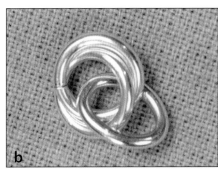

Instructions

1 Open six 5.5 mm rings and one twisted ring, and close one oval ring. These will make one complete status link component.

2 Insert an open 5.5 mm ring through the closed oval ring. Close the ring (**a**).

3 Insert a second 5.5 mm ring through the closed 5.5 mm ring and through the oval ring. Close the ring (**b**). These two 5.5 mm rings form a "flower." Run a wire tie through the flower. Twist the ends of the wire closed.

4 Insert a 5.5 mm ring through the first oval ring and through a second closed oval ring. Repeat step 3 with another 5.5 mm ring, but run it through the new oval ring as well (**c**).

5 Place a smooth open ring around the oval ring as shown (**d**). Close the ring (**e**).

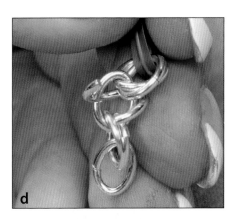

6 Repeat step 5 with a twisted ring, placing it above the smooth ring you just added (**f**).

Add another smooth ring, repeating step 5 but placing this ring above the twisted ring as shown (**g**). Push the rings down over the middle of the oval ring. Adjust as needed. You have completed one component.

7 Repeat steps 2–6, always attaching to the end oval, until the chain reaches the desired length (**h**).

8 Attach the clasp to the last flower on each end of the bracelet using the 18-gauge 3.5 mm rings (**i**).

Note: You can make a matching pair of earrings by building one component per earring and attaching the component to an earring finding with an 18-gauge 3.5 mm ring.

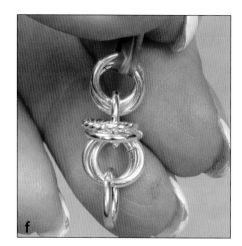

Dreaming in Mail Set

This suite of bracelet and earrings are a staple in my jewelry wardrobe. Use crystals, stones, pearls, and other types of round beads to customize the look to match your style.

Materials

Bracelet
- Sterling silver rings
  - **28** 18-gauge 6.5 mm ID, 4 rings per in. (2 rings per cm)
  - **84** 18-gauge 3.5 mm ID, 12 rings per in. (5 rings per cm)
  - **20** 20-gauge 4.0 mm ID
- **14** 6 mm crystal rondelles
- **28** 2 mm sterling silver round beads
- **12** in. (30 cm) beading wire, .014 or finer
- **2** sterling silver crimp tubes
- **2** Wire Guards
- Clasp

Note: The silver beads help to fill in the flat spaces on each side of the crystal rondelles and hold them straight. For rondelle-shaped stones or beads, omit the silver beads. You can also make the bracelet with 4 mm beads or crystals instead of the rondelles.

Earrings
- Sterling silver rings
  - **4** 18-gauge 6.5 mm ID
  - **14** 18-gauge 3.5 mm ID
- **2** 6 mm crystal rondelles
- **4** 2 mm sterling silver round beads
- **2** 1½ in. (3.8 cm) 22-gauge head pins
- Pair of earring findings

Tools
- Chainnose pliers
- Flatnose pliers
- Wire cutter
- Crimping pliers
- Wire tie or artistic wire

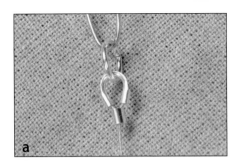

a

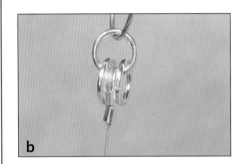

b

c

d   e

Note: Thick beading wire does not fit down the center of the chain. Fine or extra-fine works best. If you use beading wire only, the end of the wire can wear through as it rubs against the jump ring. Wire Guards help protect the wire.

Instructions

Bracelet

1. String a crimp tube on a 12-in. (30 cm) piece of beading wire, and go through both sides of a Wire Guard and back through the crimp tube. Crimp the crimp tube and trim any excess wire on the short tail.

2. Run an open 20-gauge 4.0 mm ring through the Wire Guard and close the ring. Run a wire tie through the closed ring and twist the ends closed (**a**).

3. Open two 20-gauge rings. Run each one through the 20-gauge ring that is on the wire, being sure to place a ring on each side of the beading wire. Close each ring as you place it (**b**).

4. Open two more 20-gauge rings. Run each ring through the last two rings placed and through the Wire Guard, being sure to place a ring on each side of the beading wire. Close the rings as you place them (**c**).

5. Open two 18-gauge 3.5 mm rings. Run a ring through the last two rings in the chain and close the ring. Run a second ring through the same two rings on the other side of the wire. Close the ring (**d**). While building the chain, always keep the beading wire down the middle of the chain, placing rings on either side of the wire. You will use only 18-gauge rings from now on until you reach the end of the chain.

6 Place two more 18-gauge 3.5 mm rings through the last two rings on each side of the wire. Close the rings.

Repeat with two more 18-gauge 3.5 mm rings, going through the last two rings in the chain (**e**). You will now have a chain that is eleven rings long, or a 1-2-2-2-2-2 chain.

7 Flip the last two rings down and put them between your thumb and first finger to create "bunny ears" as shown (**f**).

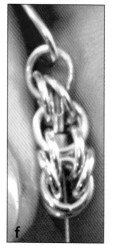

8 Run an 18-gauge 6.5 mm open ring, through the bottom edge of the bunny ears and close the ring. This locks the bunny ears in place. Run a second open 18-gauge 6.5 mm ring through the bottom edge of the bunny ears on the other side of the beading wire (**g**). Close the ring.

9 String a silver round bead, a crystal rondelle, and a second silver bead on the beading wire (**h**). (If using a rondelle-shaped bead or a crystal, you don't need to use the silver beads.)

10 Push the silver beads and rondelle inside the 6.5 mm rings (**i**).

11 Run an 18-gauge 3.5 mm ring through the two large rings and close it. Run a second ring of the same size through the same two rings on the other side of the beading wire and close it (**j**). These two rings trap the silver beads and the crystal rondelle inside the larger rings.

12 Add two more 3.5 mm rings through the last two rings and close them. Add a second set of 3.5 mm rings and close them. You now have a 2-2-2 chain of 3.5 mm rings (**k**). After you see a 2-2-2 chain like this, repeat step 7 to create bunny ears.

13 Repeat steps 7–12 until you reach the desired length. You will need 12–15 rondelle segments. Place a set of 3.5 mm rings through the last set of 6.5 mm rings. Run the beading wire through a crimp and a Wire Guard, looping the wire through the crimp a second time. Crimp the crimp tube and trim the excess wire (**l**).

14 Place a second set of 3.5 mm rings through the last two rings. The crimp is now inside those rings (**m**).

15 Begin using the 20-gauge 4.0 mm rings again. Place two of the 4.0 mm rings on either side of the Wire Guard and through the two end rings. Close the rings. You now have a 2-2-2 chain extending from the large rings.

16 Run two more 4.0 mm rings through the end rings, and run at least one of them through the Wire Guard. You now have a 2-2-2-2 chain extending from the 6.5 mm rings (**n**).

Note: You may find that you are able to run the rings in step 15 through the Wire Guard, instead of running the

rings in step 16 through the Wire Guard. You can do this in either step.

17 Add another pair of 4.0 mm rings to make the chain a 2-2-2-2-2 chain (**o**).

18 Remove the wire tie from the beginning of the chain. Open the first ring and run it through one half of the clasp. Close the ring. You may need to add another ring to this end of the chain before attaching your clasp, if the clasp does not lie correctly. Finish with a single ring through the rings on the other end of the chain and also through the clasp. You may need to add one more ring to ensure the clasp lies correctly.

Try using round gemstones, glass beads, or crystals in any color (or colors) you like. These bracelets and earrings make great gifts.

k

l

m

n

o

Earrings

1 Open five and close two 18-gauge 3.5 mm rings (small) and open two 18-gauge 6.5 mm rings (large).

2 Insert a small ring through the two closed rings and close the ring. Insert a second small ring through the same path and close the ring. You will have a 2-2 chain (**p**).

3 Insert a small ring through the last two rings and close the ring. Run a second small ring through the same path and close the ring. You will have a 2-2-2 chain (**q**).

4 Flip the end two rings down and hold them between your thumb and first finger (**r**).

5 Split the end rings apart and run a large ring through the inside rings, which are between the split rings (**s**). Close the ring.

6 Run a second large ring through the same path and close the ring (**t**).

7 String a silver round bead, a crystal rondelle, and a silver bead on a head pin. Run the head pin through the center of the rings on the chain (**u**). You will have to work the rings to get the head pin through. Move the silver beads and rondelle to the inside of the two large rings (**v**).

8 Wrap the end of the head pin around the bottom edge of one of the end small rings to tie it off (**w**).

9 Trim the excess wire off the head pin. Place a single small ring through the last two small rings on the end of the chain, and run it through the earring finding. Close the ring (**x**).

Note: Be sure to arrange the cut end of the wire on the head pin toward the back of the earring so it isn't noticeable when you wear it.

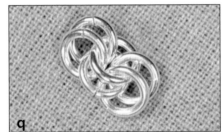

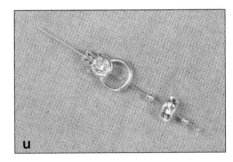

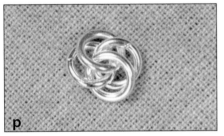

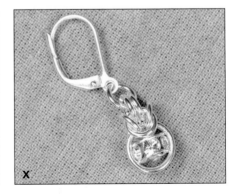

Crazy Eight Set

A wonderful combination of color and silver, this original weave has "trapped" crystals within a cage of rings. I named the weave Crazy Eight because the crystal segments resemble the number eight and the rolling rings add a crazy touch to the chain.

Materials

Bracelet
- Sterling silver rings
  - **72** 18-gauge 6.0 mm ID, 8 rings per in. (4 rings per cm)
  - **7** 18-gauge 3.0 mm ID
  - **7** 18-gauge 4.2 x 6.5 mm ID oval
  - **21** 12-gauge 6.5 mm ID, 3 rings per in. (2 rings per cm)
- **12** 6 mm round crystals
- Clasp

Note: Be sure to use a round crystal, as other shapes (such as bicones) tend to fall through the cage.

Necklace, 40 in. (102 cm)
- Sterling silver rings
  - **312** 18-gauge 6.0 mm ID, 8 rings per in. (4 rings per cm)
  - **39** 18-gauge 3.0 mm ID
  - **39** 18-gauge 4.2 x 6.5 mm ID oval
  - **117** 12-gauge 6.5 mm ID, 3 rings per in. (2 rings per cm)
- **78** 6 mm round crystals
- Clasp

Earrings
- Sterling silver rings
  - **16** 18-gauge 6.0 mm ID
  - **4** 18-gauge 3.0 mm ID
  - **2** 22-gauge 2.0 mm ID
- **4** 6 mm round crystals
- Pair of earring findings

Tools
- Chainnose pliers
- Flatnose pliers
- Wire tie or artistic wire

a

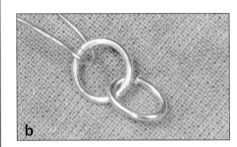

b

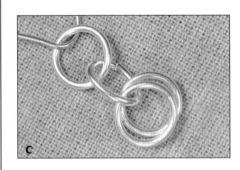

c

d

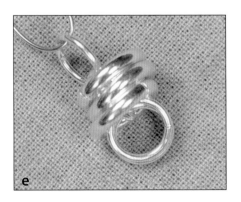

e

Instructions

Bracelet and Necklace

1 Open nine 18-gauge 6.0 mm rings and one oval ring.

2 Close a 6.0 mm ring and place it on a wire tie. Twist the end of the wire closed (**a**).

3 Run an open oval ring through the end ring and close the ring (**b**).

Note: The oval rings do not always close with as nice a join as a round ring, but do not worry too much about that. The oval ring will be surrounded with 12-gauge rings, and the join will not show.

4 Run an open 6.0 mm ring through the oval ring and close the ring. Run a second 6.0 mm ring through the same path and close the ring. You now have a 1-1-2 chain (**c**).

5 Open a 12-gauge ring and run it around the oval ring. Close the ring (**d**). (The new ring fits around the oval and does not fall off the end of the chain because the 6.0 mm rings block it.)

6 Repeat step 5 with two more 12-gauge rings (**e**). As you are placing these rings, keep pulling the oval ring so it lies lengthwise between the 18-gauge rings on each of its ends. The oval will try to slip sideways, so continue to adjust it until you have all three 12-gauge rings on and closed.

7 Run two open 6.0 mm rings through the two end rings, closing each ring as you go (**f**). Open a 3.0 mm ring and place it on your mat.

8 While holding the chain between your fingers, spread the end two rings apart (**g**). You are forming a space for the crystal, which you will place in the next step.

9 Spread the two inside rings apart place a round crystal in the space formed by the four rings (**h**). Hold the rings and crystal in place with your fingers. You may need to pull the last two rings so they lie one on each side of the connecting oval ring where it is attached to the first two 6.0 mm rings.

10 Run the open 3.0 mm ring from your mat through the two end rings (**i**). Close the ring. The crystal is now trapped in the four-ring cage (**j**).

11 Run two 6.0 mm rings through the 3.0 mm ring on the end. Run two more 6.0 mm rings through the two end rings (**k**).

12 Repeat steps 8–9, trapping another crystal. Repeat step 10, using an open oval ring (**l**) instead of the 3.0 mm ring. The pattern is now beginning to repeat.

13 As you did in step 4, run two 6.0 mm rings through the oval ring (**m**).

Repeat the pattern from steps 7–13, forming another crystal segment and another oval ring segment. Then add three of the 12-gauge rings as in steps 5–6. Continue repeating these steps for the length of the bracelet.

14 When the chain is the desired length, remove the wire tie and attach one half of your clasp on that end by opening the end ring and running it through the clasp (**n**).

For a lobster claw clasp, use the end ring to clasp the bracelet. For a toggle, attach the second half of the clasp to the remaining end ring.

Earrings

1 Open eight 6.0 mm rings, two 3.0 mm rings, and one 2.0 mm ring.

2 Run a 3.0 mm ring through the earring finding loop and close the ring (**o**).

3 Run a 6.0 mm ring through the end ring and close the ring. Run a second ring through the same path and close the ring (**p**).

4 Run a 6.0 mm ring through the pair of 6.0 mm rings and close it. Repeat with a second 6.0 mm ring. You now have a 1-2-2 chain (**q**).

5 Follow steps 8–11 in "Bracelet and Necklace."

6 Follow steps 8–10, using a 2.0 mm ring instead of a 3.0 mm ring in step 10 to close the end of the earrings (**r**).

Repeat to make a second earring.

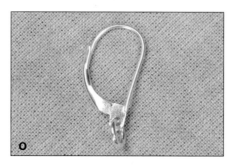

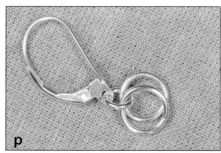

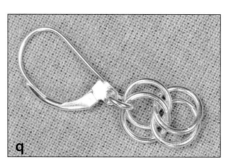

Sassy Swirl of Rings Set

Fresh and modern, these pieces truly flow along the wrist, neck, or face. The Sassy Swirl of Rings jewelry suite is a quick, easy way to draw attention with loads of bright, shiny jump rings.

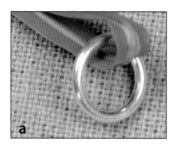

a

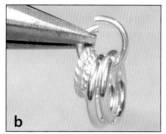

b

c.

d

Materials

Bracelet
- Sterling silver rings
  - **35** 16-gauge 5.0 mm ID, 5 rings per in. (2 rings per cm)
  - **72** 16-gauge 6.5 mm ID, 10 rings per in. (4 rings per cm), including two for connecting the clasp
  - **70** 18-gauge 4.25 mm ID twisted, 10 rings per in. (4 rings per cm)
- Clasp

Necklace, 18 in. (45.7 cm) adjustable
- Sterling silver rings
  - **142** 16-gauge 6.5 mm ID, 10 rings per in. (4 rings per cm)
  - **85** 16-gauge 5.0 mm ID, 5 rings per in. (2 rings per cm), including 15 rings for the necklace extender
  - **140** 18-gauge 4.25 mm ID twisted, 10 rings per in. (4 rings per cm)
- Lobster claw clasp

Earrings
- Sterling silver rings
  - **16** 16-gauge 6.5 mm ID
  - **6** 16-gauge 5.0 mm ID
  - **2** 18-gauge 3.5 mm
  - **16** 18-gauge 4.25 mm ID twisted
- Pair of earring findings

Tools
- Chainnose pliers
- Flatnose pliers
- Wire tie or artistic wire

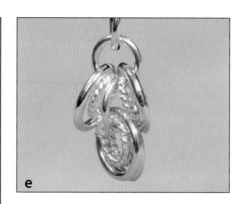

e

f

Instructions

Bracelet

1 Close one 16-gauge 5.0 mm ring (connector ring) and open six other connector rings. Close four 16-gauge 6.5 mm (large) rings and close four twisted rings. Continue to open and close rings as needed throughout the pattern.

2 Place the closed connector ring on a wire tie. Twist the end of the wire closed (**a**).

3 Pick up an open connector ring and scoop up two closed large rings and two closed twisted rings. Do not close the connector ring (**b**).

4 Run the open connector ring through the closed ring on the wire. Close the connector ring (**c**).

5 Separate the rings as shown (**d**). Place a large and twisted ring on the left, and a large and twisted ring on the right.

g

h

i

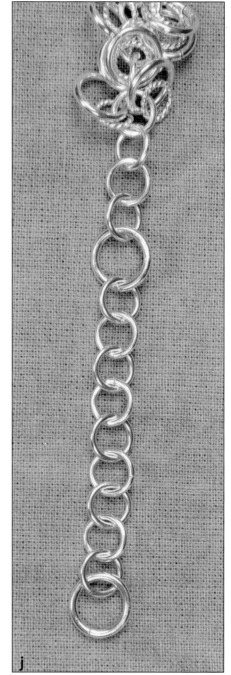

j

6 With an open connector ring, pick up two closed large rings and two closed twisted rings. Run the open connector ring through the bottom connector ring of the chain, positioning the new ring between the two sets of large and twisted rings.

7 Close the connector ring. The set (two large and two twisted rings per set) should hang from the chain as shown (e).

8 Continue adding sets of large and twisted rings with a connector ring through the last connector ring and between the last set of large and twisted rings (f).

9 When the chain is the desired length, open the beginning ring (the one on the wire) and attach one half of the clasp to the end ring (g). Attach the other half of the clasp to the other end of the bracelet, going through the last connector ring and again between the two sets of large and twisted rings. (For a lobster claw clasp, use a new ring.)

Necklace

1 Close a 5.0 mm ring and run a wire tie through it. Twist the ends of the wire tie closed.

2 Open two 5.0 mm rings. Run an open 5.0 mm ring through the closed 5.0 mm ring and close the ring. Run the other open 5.0 mm through the last ring and close it. You now have a 1-1-1 chain (h).

3 Repeat steps 3–8 in "Bracelet" until you have used all of the 6.5 mm rings (except for two for the extender) and the 4.25 mm rings. This section should be built off the 1-1-1 chain (i). When you have used all the rings, you should have about 14 in. (35.6 cm) of chain, not including the three-ring chain.

4 Make a 1-1-1 chain with 5.0 mm rings off the last 5.0 mm connector ring at the end of your chain. Run an open 6.5 mm ring through the end ring and close the ring. Continue building a 1-1 chain with nine 5.0 mm rings off the end 6.5 mm ring. Finally, run an open 6.5 mm ring through the end 5.0 mm ring of the chain and close the ring (j).

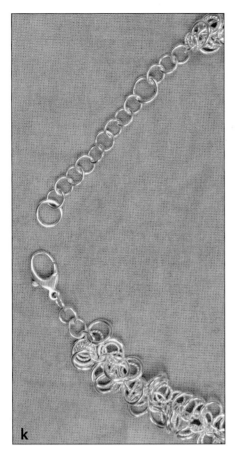

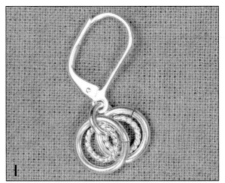

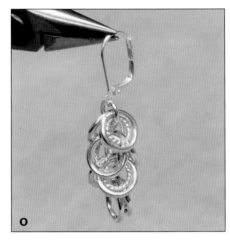

5 Remove the wire from the end of the chain. Open the end 5.0 mm ring and attach your lobster claw clasp to it. Close the ring (**k**).

The extender chain allows you to adjust the length from 16–18 in. (41–46 cm). This necklace can also be made longer by adding more 5.0 mm rings and another 6.5 mm end ring to the chain.

Earrings

1 Open three 16-gauge 5.0 mm rings (connector rings). Close eight 16-gauge 6.5 mm (large) rings and close eight twisted rings. Open an 18-gauge 3.5 mm ring.

2 Scoop up two closed large rings and two closed twisted rings (this is a set of rings) with the 3.5 mm ring. Do not close the ring.

3 Run the 3.5 mm ring through the earring finding. Close the ring (**l**). Separate the rings as shown (**m**). You want to have a large and twisted ring on the left, and a large and twisted ring on the right.

4 Repeat step 2 using a 5.0 mm connector ring instead of a 3.5 mm ring. Run the 5.0 mm ring through the 3.5 mm ring, positioning the new ring between the two sets of large and twisted rings (**n**).

5 Repeat step 4 twice, running the new 5.0 mm ring through the last 5.0 mm ring in the chain. You now have four sets of large and twisted ring pairs along the length of the earring (**o**).

Repeat to make a second earring. You can make the earrings longer or shorter by adding or subtracting sets of rings.

From the Author

I began my professional career as a registered nurse. Throughout the years I have been involved in handcrafts such as knitting, needlepoint, crocheting, and eventually beading. One day I saw a class for a Byzantine bracelet in a local bead store. I took that class and my beading days were over! I took other chain mail classes for a year or so, but then began to branch out and develop my own designs. My original designs have been published in beading magazines. Over time, I started teaching chain mail classes at local bead stores and later went on to teach at national shows. My love for chain mail just continues to grow.

I hope that you have found the information in this book useful. I also hope that you have enjoyed making the many different weaves. As I often tell the students in my classes, making chain mail jewelry can be addicting. You can never seem to get enough. Please take what I have shared, and develop the weaves into other variations that will be beautiful in their own right. For more information, kits, and rings, you can visit my Web site, jewelrybysueonline.com. Happy chain mailling!

I would like to thank my husband and partner in chain mailling and in life, Steve, for all of his support and understanding. He is terrific when I am focused on making and developing new weaves and variations of weaves. Steve makes the best jump rings for chain mail that are available. I could not make the beautiful jewelry that I do without them. Thank you so much!

Also, thank you to my daughter, Megan, my son, Matt, and my mother, Mary, for their understanding of my love for chain mail and the time it takes. They are great critics concerning my new patterns and offer wonderful suggestions for improving them. I also receive much enjoyment from Devon and Logan, my twin grandsons. They are very interested in "Nana Sue's" tools and rings. Maybe someday they will also make chain mail.

Finally, thank you to all of the students I have taught over the years. Their enthusiasm for chain mail has been a joy for me to experience. I am honored to be able to be a part of their lives for a brief moment in time.

Gauges and Inner Diameters

The term "ID" stands for "inner diameter," and it is literally the diameter of the inside of a jump ring measured in millimeters (mm). The gauge of a jump ring is the thickness of the wire that is used to make the jump ring. Why are these important? The gauge and the ID of a jump ring affect how the rings will fit in a specific piece of jewelry. If you use jump rings with the wrong ID or gauge, the weave may be too tight or too loose. The chart below shows the ID and the gauge of jump rings in the common sizes used in chain mail jewelry. If you have a jump ring of unknown gauge or ID, you can lay it on the chart and figure out its size.

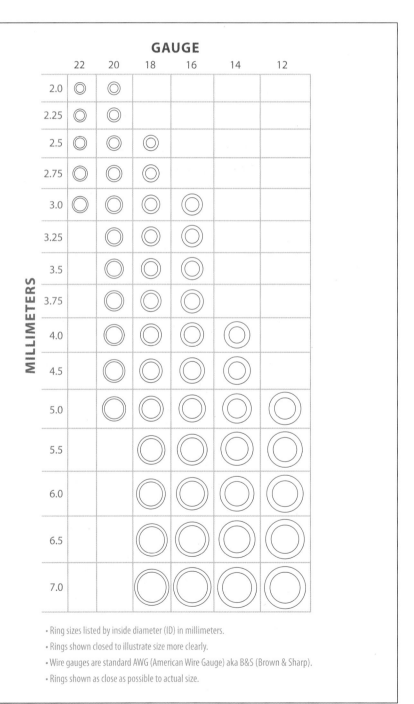

- Ring sizes listed by inside diameter (ID) in millimeters.
- Rings shown closed to illustrate size more clearly.
- Wire gauges are standard AWG (American Wire Gauge) aka B&S (Brown & Sharp).
- Rings shown as close as possible to actual size.